NAVY Trivia

by
Paul E. Kanive

Copyright © by
Quinlan Press, Inc.
All rights reserved,
including the right of reproduction
in whole or in part in any form.
Published by Quinlan Press, Inc.
131 Beverly Street
Boston, MA 02114
(617) 227-4870

Cover design by Henry Quinlan

Library of Congress Catalog Card Number
85-63123
ISBN 0-933341-27-X

First printing March 1986

DEDICATION

To the "Mets"
(33rd Company, US Naval Academy,
Class of 1967)
... especially
Gregg Owens
John Harrington
Naval Aviators gone from us too soon ...

ACKNOWLEDGEMENTS

In any effort such as this, a significant undertaking is providing credit to the many and diverse sources of information. The selected bibliography is but a portion of the references consulted. Issues of various Navy-oriented periodicals have proved invaluable, especially: **All Hands, Naval Aviation News** and **Surface Warfare** magazines.

Special thanks to Mrs. Jane Price of the US Naval Academy (Nimitz Library) and Mrs. Patty M. Maddocks, Director of the Naval Institute Library, for their assistance in this project.

All photographs appear courtesy the Naval Academy, the Naval Institute and the Defense Audiovisual Agency, Washington DC.

My deepest gratitude is offered to a close friend and classmate, Mike Quinlan, of the Quinlan Publishing Company in Boston, who initially conceived the idea of this modest effort and made it happen.

Paul Kanive is a graduate of the US Naval Academy, where he played battalion football and company fieldball and sang baritone in the academy choir. A naval flight officer, he flew 309 F-4 combat missions with Fighter Squadron 114 from the USS **Kitty Hawk** (CV-63) during the Vietnam War. He received two awards of the Air Medal (20 strike/flight) and other citations, campaign ribbons and foreign awards. Following graduate school and a tour of duty with Fighter Squadron 151, he was designated a qualified subspecialist in the field of quantitative economics while assigned to the Economic Analysis Section, Office of the Chief of Naval Operations. Commander Kanive is currently a professor of management teaching, decision making and resource allocation at the Naval War College, Newport, Rhode Island.

Table of Contents

CONFLICTS 1
   ANSWERS 19

PERSONALITIES 33
   ANSWERS 61

NAVY LORE 71
   ANSWERS 85

HISTORY 97
   ANSWERS 139

GENERAL 161
   ANSWERS 189

CONFLICTS

1. Name the only US aircraft carrier lost in the Atlantic during World War II.

2. **U-656,** the first German submarine sunk by US forces in World War II, fell victim to what kind of aircraft?

3. In World War I the main role of the US Navy's Flying Corps in Europe was to undertake anti-U-boat patrols with Curtiss long-range flying boats from twenty-seven bases in France, England, Ireland, the Azores and Italy, in addition to twelve bases on the US coast. The first attack made on an enemy submarine occurred when, and who was the pilot involved?

4. The first occasion that a US aircraft was fired upon (and hit) in anger occurred prior to World War I. What was the conflict, and who was the pilot?

5. How did the Navy lose the only lighter-than-air airship that was lost during World War II?

Conflicts—Questions

6. What World War II engagement became known as the "Great Turkey Shoot"?

7. What World War II battle is considered to be the greatest naval battle in history?

8. Identify the first US Naval Aviator in history to shoot down an enemy jet aircraft.

9. What was the first Japanese aircraft carrier sunk during World War II?

10. During which World War II engagement did US Navy combatants first encounter the "Divine Wind," Japanese kamikaze aircraft?

11. The first Japanese ship sunk by the US in World War II was sunk by which US submarine?

12. Who was the first Navy flag officer killed in World War II?

13. Identify the only US submarine to sink a battleship in World War II.

14. Japan's first ever naval defeat occurred during World War II. What battle accounted for this defeat?

15. Name the first naval battle in which no ship of either side sighted one of the other's—the fighting was done by carrier aircraft against carrier aircraft, or carrier aircraft against ship.

16. The last sea battle of the Revolutionary War was fought 10 March 1783. Name the ships involved.

Conflicts—Questions

17. The war with Japan ended on 2 September 1945. Where was the Peace Treaty signed?

18. Name the US combatant whose casualties totaled over half those suffered by the entire fleet on 7 December 1941. The ship, which has never been formally decommissioned, now rests on the bottom of Pearl Harbor.

19. To which Pacific island chain does the term "Ironbottom Sound" have special significance?

20. Identify the noted public servant who was the youngest Naval Aviator in the Navy (he won his wings in 1942 at the age of eighteen) and flew TBM Avengers from the USS **San Jacinto**. He was shot down on his fifty-eigth mission, rescued by the USS **Finback** (SS-230) and awarded the Distinguished Flying Cross for his actions.

21. What US Navy submarine not only sunk more Japanese ships than any other sub (twenty-six) but was also present during the attack on Pearl Harbor and credited with downing the first Japanese aircraft during the attack on 7 December 1941?

22. For the first time since 1815, an American naval vessel captured and boarded a foreign man-of-war on the high seas 4 June 1944. Identify the foreign man-of-war.

Conflicts—Questions

23. Thirty-four year-old Yale graduate David Bushnell built a vessel named **Turtle**—what was unique about this ship?

24. Bushnell continued his pioneering endeavors to complicate the British presence in America. In 1778 he was a prime mover in the "Battle of the Kegs" on the Delaware River. What was his new invention, and what were the results?

25. Identify the site of the first American amphibious operation.

26. Who became the first Naval Aviator to score victories over five enemy jet aircraft?

27. On May Day, 1951, aircraft from the USS **Princeton** (CV-37) attacked the Hwachon Dam in Korea. What was unusual about this strike?

28. Identify the first two aces of the Vietnam War, who were also the first F-4 Phantom aces, the first aviators to destroy three MiGs in one aerial engagement and the first all-missile aces (all opponents downed with air-to-air missiles)?

29. Who is credited with the first air-to-air victory of the Vietnam conflict?

30. What was the first war in which underwater explosions effectively sank ships?

31. What US combatant was attacked in the first Gulf of Tonkin Incident in August of 1964?

Conflicts—Questions

32. Navy F-4 Phantom II aircraft from which US aircraft carrier made the first and last MiG kills of the Vietnam War on 17 June 1965 and 12 January 1973 respectively?

33. What was the first use of airborne minesweepers to counter "live" mines?

34. What two aircraft carriers launched air strikes against North Vietnamese torpedo boats and supporting facilities on 5 August 1964 in response to the Gulf of Tonkin Incident?

35. What was "Rolling Thunder" during the Vietnam War?

36. What were the only two Navy air units stationed in-country during the Vietnam War?

37. What was Operation Pocket Money during the Vietnam War?

38. What was the last war in which ramming was seriously considered a naval tactic?

39. What event marked the first US victory in the first international conflict since the Mexican War?

40. What was the name for the World War II campaign against German and Italian U-boat attacks on allied trade at sea?

41. When and where was the US Navy's first surface battle after 1898?

Conflicts—Questions

42. On the morning of 7 December 1941, the Japanese air raid on Pearl Harbor sank how many of the seven battleships moored along "Battleship Row"?

43. How many US battleships were located at Pearl Harbor the morning of 7 December 1941?

44. What was the first US naval vessel destroyed by the Axis powers in 1941?

45. What World War II battle, in which the Japanese lost four aircraft carriers, was considered the turning point of the war in the Pacific?

46. During World War II the regular nighttime movement of Japanese naval units down the "Slot" through the Central Solomons to reinforce and resupply troops on Guadalcanal became known by what name?

47. What was the first major warship sunk by a US submarine in World War II?

48. What World War II Navy aircraft were given the nickname "Black Cats"?

49. True or False: On 23 February 1942 the oil refinery at Ellwood, near Santa Barbara, California, was shelled by a Japanese destroyer.

50. How did Gen. Douglas MacArthur escape from Corregidor?

51. What was the first carrier air battle fought?

Confilcts—Questions

52. Of the 130 Japanese submarines sunk during World War II, approximately how many were sunk by American submarines?

53. Name the first Naval Aviator to shoot down an enemy aircraft.

54. What US aircraft carrier absorbed the most punishment and casualties from the Japanese and still remained afloat?

55. How did the Navy assist the Army in crossing the Rhine River in March of 1945?

56. Operation Iceberg was the code name for what famous World War II undertaking?

57. What was the last sortie of the Imperial Japanese Navy?

58. What were "Hydeman's Hellcats"?

59. What was the bloodiest battle in the history of the US Navy?

60. Kikusui—floating chrysanthemums in Japanese—was used to describe what Japanese action?

61. What was the most effective anti-ship weapon the Japanese used in World War II?

62. What was the only US naval vessel to surrender in World War II?

Conflicts—Questions

63. During World War II what was the ABDA command?

64. What two US combatants achieved the first U-boat kill of World War I?

65. Name the first Navy man killed in action in World War I.

66. Commanded by Rear Adm. Albert Gleaves, what function did the Cruiser and Transport Force perform in World War I?

67. What were the last shots of the Spanish-American War?

68. Name the only major US Navy combatant lost in World War I.

69. When and who fired the first shots of the Spanish-American War?

70. Employed during the Vietnam War, what was Operation Game Warden?

71. First used by the US Navy in 1966, what was a PBR?

72. What were known as "Kaiser's coffins"?

73. What US Navy ship had the misfortune to be the first to take a direct hit from a North Vietnamese shore battery?

74. Name the two Navy hospital ships that each spent four years supporting US efforts in Vietnam between 1966 and 1971.

Conflicts—Questions

75. Name the top three scoring US submarines in World War II (on the basis of enemy ships sunk).

76. What US submarine is credited with firing the last torpedoes and sinking the last Japanese combatant ships in World War II?

77. Name the only naval officer killed in the Spanish-American War.

78. Whose report of action during the Battle of Santiago on 3 July 1898 opened with the following: "The fleet under my command offers the nation as a Fourth of July present the whole of Cervera's fleet"?

79. What started the war with Tripoli in 1801?

80. What was the Chesapeake-Leopard Affair?

81. What was the only strictly naval action involving a US warship during the Korean War?

82. On 11 July 1950 the railway tunnel at Rashin, North Korea, was destroyed by a raid from what US Navy ship?

83. What was the first US Navy vessel lost in the Korean War?

84. True or False: Navy aircraft of Task Force 77 were ordered to attack only the Korean end of Yalu River bridges linking China and North Korea.

Conflicts—Questions

85. Extremely popular with Eighth Army, what were the "Cherokee Strikes" of the Korean War?

86. What World War II US submarine holds the record for the most Japanese submarines sunk in the fewest days?

87. Of what significance was the Battle of Vella Gulf in August of 1943?

88. How many American destroyers were sunk by U-boats during World War II?

89. Who was the first American prisoner of war in the Vietnam War?

90. During the Vietnam War, what was Operation Market Time?

91. What US Navy ship delivered the first naval gunfire support of the Korean War?

92. How many US destroyers were lost during the Okinawa campaign?

93. What Navy action stopped the seaborne flow of supplies to North Vietnam virtually overnight?

94. When and where was the agreement signed which ended direct American participation in the Vietnam War?

95. Identify the US Navy's last in-country combat unit during the Vietnam War.

Conflicts—Questions

96. How many of the attacking Japanese midget submarines were sunk in the attack on Pearl Harbor?

97. What was the only successful operation carried out by the ABDA (American-British-Dutch-Australian) command in World War II?

98. What was the first naval action in which the US Navy coordinated surface, submarine and aircraft units in a night bombardment?

99. What World War II warrior originated the following: "Thirty-one knot Burke get athwart the Buka-Rabaul evacuation line about 35 miles west of Buka X If no enemy contacts by 0300 . . . 25th . . . come south to refuel same place X If enemy contacted you know what to do"?

100. What was the Ohka or "Baka" bomb?

101. What accounted for most of the ninety-nine destroyers lost in the Second World War?

102. What US combatant was the first to engage a unit of the Japanese attacking force the morning of 7 December 1941?

103. What naval officer was the weaponeer on the B-29 known as "Enola Gay" on 6 August 1945?

104. Who was the first flag officer killed in the Vietnam War?

Conflicts—Questions

105. Name the first three American POWs released by the North Vietnamese 5 August 1969.

106. What was the Brown-Water Navy in the Vietnam War?

107. True or False: During World War I about twenty US subs reached the war zone—with some of those serving in European waters encountering German U-boats. No kills were, however, credited to the Americans.

108. How many personnel losses did the Navy experience in World War I when it carried and convoyed well over 1.5 million men to Europe?

109. Compared to the earlier problem-prone submarine torpedoes, what was different about the Mark 18 torpedo used by US subs from June 1943 onward?

110. The attributes of good range, fire power and seaworthiness made the 175 ship _____ class DDs the best all-round destroyers of World War II.

111. What World War II destroyer was known as the "Blue Beetle" as a result of her unusual camouflage?

112. What was the first enemy submarine sunk by the US Navy?

113. What was unique about the flag used as a backdrop for the signing table at the

Conflicts—Questions

Japanese surrender ceremony onboard the USS **Missouri** (BB-63) 2 September 1945?

114. How many US presidents were on Navy duty during World War II, and what were their ranks?

115. The submarine snorkel was first used operationally in World War II by what country's navy?

116. Name the UH-2 Seasprite pilot who became the first Naval Aviator to receive the Medal of Honor in Vietnam.

117. Upon seeing the Kwajalein battlefield for the first time, what famous naval officer remarked to his staff: "It's the worst devastation I've ever seen except for that last Texas picnic in Honolulu"?

118. Considered to be among the most effective operations of the Vietnam War, the mining of the Haiphong Harbor channel in May of 1972 trapped what number of major merchant ships for the duration of the war?

119. Name the counterpart for Tokyo Rose who did her broadcasting from Berlin.

120. What event triggered the war John Hay referred to as "a splendid little war"—the Spanish American War?

121. What North Vietnamese bridge was referred to as the "Dragon's Jaw"?

Conflicts—Questions

122. When and what was the first enemy naval vessel sunk by a US Navy submarine?

123. Allied anti-submarine efforts accounted for how many German submarines in the Battle of the Atlantic?

124. On 24 April 1917 the first flotilla of six US destroyers departed for Europe under the command of Cdr. J.K. Taussig. Name three of the destroyers involved.

125. What was the total number of US destroyers that served in Europe from 1917-18?

126. What is the name of this vessel?

Conflicts—Questions

127. For what were these aircraft used?

15

Conflicts—Questions

128. What is the name of this vessel, and in what battle is it engaged?

Conflicts—Questions

129. What is the name of this vessel, and why is she famous?

17

ANSWERS

1. The USS **Block Island** (CVE-21), which was torpedoed by a German U-boat 29 May 1944

2. Lockheed **Hudson**, PBO piloted by Ensign W. Tepuni of VP-82 on 1 March 1942.

3. 25 March 1918; Ens. John F. McNamara

4. Vera Cruz operations during the war with Mexico (6 May 1914); Lt. (jg) P.N.L. Bellinger, with Ens. W.D. LaMont as observer

5. Airship K-74 was shot down by a German U-boat off the Florida Keys 18 July 1943.

6. The first phase of the Battle of the Philippine Sea was a series of air engagements, most noticeable was the "Great Marianas Turkey Shoot" in which Japan lost 346 aircraft and two carriers as opposed to US losses of thirty aircraft.

Conflicts—Answers

7. The Battle for Leyte Gulf

8. Lcdr. W.T. Amen, CO Fighter Squadron III, (VF-111). While supporting the initial air strikes against Yalu River bridges in a F9F Panther, he shot down a MiG-15 in the first engagement between Navy jets and MiG aircraft on 9 November 1950.

9. **Shoho**, during the Battle of the Coral Sea 7 May 1942

10. The Battle for Leyte Gulf

11. The USS **Swordfish**. It sank the **Atsutasau Maru** on 15 December 1941.

12. Rear Adm. Isaac C. Kidd on the USS **Arizona** (7 December 1941)

13. The USS **Sealion II**, under the command of Cdr. G.T. Reich, sank the Japanese battleship **Kongo** 21 November 1944.

14. The Battle of Midway

15. The Battle of the Coral Sea (7-8 May 1942)

16. The HMS **Sybil** and the USS **Alliance**, Capt. John Barry commanding

17. On the USS **Missouri** (BB-63) in Tokyo Bay

18. The USS **Arizona** (BB-39)

19. The Solomon Islands. Ironbottom Sound was so named on account of the number of ships sunk there.

Conflicts—Answers

20. Vice President George H.W. Bush

21. The USS **Tautog**

22. The German U-Boat **U-505**. It was captured by a Guadalcanal escort carrier group commanded by Capt. Dan Gallery.

23. It was the world's first operational submarine. First used against British ships lying off the port of New York in 1776, **Turtle** attacked Lord Howe's flagship **Eagle** but was unable to attach the explosive charge to **Eagle**'s hull.

24. He invented mines—kegs of gunpowder, suspended beneath floats for bouyancy, which activated upon contact with an obstacle. Four British casualties resulted from the first attempt at minesweeping operations.

25. Vera Cruz, Mexico

26. Maj. John F. Bolt, USMC. He downed his fifth **and sixth** MiGs while operating with the Fifth Air Force in Korea 11 July 1953.

27. It marked the first and only use of aerial torpedoes in the Korean War. Destruction and damage to the flood gates, as a result of the concentrated efforts of eight Skyraiders and twelve Corsairs, released water from the reservoir into the Pukhan River and prevented Communist forces from making an easy crossing.

Conflicts—Answers

28. Lt. Randy Cunningham and Lt. (jg) Willie Driscoll downed three MiGs 10 May 1972 which, combined with earlier kills on 19 January and 8 May, qualified them as the first aces of the Vietnam War.

29. Comdr. L.C. Paige and Lcdr. J.C. Smith downed a MiG-17 on 17 June 1965 in a VF-21 F-4 Phantom II from the USS **Midway** (CV-41).

30. The American Civil War. This war also saw the first use of turret-fitted ships against broadsides, the first encounters between armored vessels and the first wide use of shells.

31. The USS **Maddox** (DD-731)

32. The USS **Midway** (CV-41)

33. Operation Endsweep, the airborne mine countermeasures off Haiphong. CH-53 Sea Stallion from HM-12 began sweeping the Haiphong shipping channel 27 February 1973.

34. The USS **Constellation** (CV-64) and the USS **Ticonderoga** (CV-14)

35. The systematic bombing of military targets throughout North Vietnam by land and sea based air.

36. HAL-3 (Helicopter Light Attack Squadron Three with armed UH-1 aircraft) and VAL-4 (Light Attack Squadron Four, equipped with OV-10)

Conflicts—Answers

provided support for riverine and other operations in the Mekong Delta.

37. A mining campaign against principal North Vietnamese ports

38. The American Civil War

39. The Battle of Manila Bay, 1 May 1898

40. The Battle of the Atlantic

41. 24 January 1942; four destroyers of DesDiv 59 attacked an anchored Japanese troop convoy off Balikpapan.

42. Four. The other three were damaged—all but the **Arizona** and **Oklahoma** were repaired and participated in the war. (The **Oklahoma** was floated but was not repaired.)

43. Eight. The **Arizona**, **Oklahoma**, **California**, **Tennessee**, **West Virginia**, **Maryland** and **Nevada** were moored along "Battleship Row"; the **Pennsylvania** was in dry dock in the Pearl Harbor Navy Yard and was among the first ships to open fire on the attacking aircraft.

44. The USS **Reuben James** (DD-245), Lcdr. H.L. Edwards commanding, was torpedoed and sunk by **U-562** on 31 October.

45. The Battle of Midway

46. The Tokyo Express

Conflicts—Answers

47. The Japanese heavy cruiser **Kako** was sunk 10 August 1942 by the **S-44**.

48. PBY Catalinas that operated primarily at night. Too slow for day combat, the Black Cats were very useful for night bombing, searches and attacks on enemy shipping.

49. False. The Ellwood refinery was shelled by the Japanese submarine **I-17**.

50. General MacArthur, his family and some members of his staff escaped aboard units of Motor Torpedo Boat Squadron 3, Lt. John D. Bulkeley commanding.

51. The Battle of the Coral Sea (May 1942)

52. At least twenty-three

53. Ens. Stephen Potter. He downed a German seaplane over the North Sea on 19 March 1918. Potter was shot down five weeks later while engaged with seven German aircraft near Felixstowe, England.

54. The USS **Franklin** (CV-13)

55. Four boat units consisting of 218 officers and men, with twenty-four LCVP (landing craft, vehicle personnel), under Comdr. W.J. Whiteside, performed river crossings. In a two week period Boat Unit I ferried 14,000 troops and 400 vehicles across the Rhine at Bad Neuenahr.

Conflicts—Answers

56. The invasion of Okinawa (April 1945)

57. On 7 April 1945 the Japanese battleship **Yamato**, the light cruiser **Yahagi** and eight destroyers departed for a suicide attack on the US amphibious fleet off Okinawa. The **Yamato**, the **Yahagi** and four destroyers were sunk by aircraft from Task Force 58.

58. A wolf-pack of nine US submarines, under the command of Cdr. E.T. Hydeman, sent into the Sea of Japan to attack Japanese shipping. In eleven days, twenty-eight Japanese ships were sunk and one US submarine was lost.

59. The Battle of Okinawa (4,900 killed, 4,824 wounded, 32 vessels sunk and 368 vessels damaged)

60. Mass kamikaze attacks. Japanese pilots flew deliberate suicide missions which terminated when they flew their aircraft into a US ship.

61. The kamikaze

62. The Yangtze River gunboat **Wake** (PG-43). On 8 December 1941 at Shanghai, China, **Wake** struck her flag and surrendered to the Japanese following an unsuccessful attempt to scuttle the ship.

63. The unified American, British, Dutch and Australian Command. Activated 15 January 1942, Adm. T.C. Hart USN was appointed the naval commander.

Conflicts—Answers

64. The USS **Fanning** (DD-37), under the command of Lt. Arthur S. Carpenter, and the USS **Nicholson** (DD-52), under the command of Cdr. Frank D. Berrien, depth charged and sunk the **U-58**. Kapitanleutnant Gustav Amberger and the crew were rescued when the sub surfaced for the last time.

65. Gunner's Mate First Class Osmond K. Ingram. He was blown overboard from the USS **Cassin** (DD-43) by the impact of a torpedo on 16 September 1917.

66. This force of forty-five transports and twenty-four cruisers moved approximately half of the American Expeditionary Force, over 900,000 soldiers, to France and England without any loss of life due to enemy action.

67. The armed lighthouse supply ship **Mangrove**, under the command of Lcdr. D.D.V. Stuart, engaged two Spanish gunboats off Caibarien, Cuba, on 14 August 1898. The Spanish hoisted a flag of truce and informed Stuart that the armistice had been signed.

68. The cruiser **San Diego** (ACR-6). It struck a mine and sank on 19 July 1918.

69. On 22 April 1898 the gunboat **Nashville** (PG-7), under the command of Cdr. Washburn Maynard, fired two shots across the bow of the Spanish freighter **Buenaventura**.

Conflicts—Answers

70. Patrol of the Mekong Delta and the Rung Sat Special Zone (the area between Saigon and the sea) was charged to the US Navy River Patrol Force Task Force 116—its activities were known as Game Warden.

71. A thirty-one-foot-long, water-jet-propelled river patrol boat used primarily in Game Warden operations.

72. World War II Liberty Ships built by Mr. H. Kaiser between 1941 and 1948.

73. The USS **O'Brien** (DD-725). It was hit twice 23 December 1966 by a North Vietnamese shore battery located approximately three miles north of Dong Hoi.

74. The **Repose** (AH-16) and the **Sanctuary** (AH-17)

75. The **Tautog** (SS-199), **Tang** (SS-563) and **Silversides** (SS-236)

76. The USS **Torsk** (SS-423). On 14 August 1945 it sank Japanese Coast Defense Vessels numbers 13 and 47.

77. Ens. Worth Bagley. He was on board the torpedo boat **Winslow** (TB-5) when it was hit by shore batteries at C'ardenas, Cuba, 11 May 1898.

78. Rear Adm. William T. Sampson

79. The pasha of Tripoli, Yusuf Karamanli, decided the amount of tribute being paid to him by the United States was inadequate and issued a declaration of war.

Conflicts—Answers

80. The British frigate **Leopard**, commanded by Capt. S.P. Humphreys, intercepted the US frigate **Chesapeake**, commanded by Capt. Charles Gordon and with Commodore James Barron on board. Captain Humphreys demanded to search the ship for British deserters. Upon Barron's refusal to permit the search, **Leopard** opened fire and forced Barron to strike **Chesapeake**'s colors. A boarding party from **Leopard** seized four crewmen. Commodore Barron was found guilty at a court martial of negligence and suspended from the Navy for five years.

81. On 2 July 1950, four North Korean torpedo boats attacked the USS **Juneau**, the HMS **Jamaica** and the HMS **Black Swan**. Three of the torpedo boats were destroyed.

82. The USS **Juneau** (CL-119). Cdr. W.B. Porter led ten seamen and marines on this first of many successful operations conducted by US naval forces.

83. Minesweeper **Magpie** (AMS-25), Lt. (jg) W.R. Person commanding, was destroyed by a mine off Chuksan, North Korea.

84. True

85. Strikes initiated by Vice Adm. J.J. "Jocko" Clark against enemy supply facilities outside the range of UN artillery. Beginning in October of 1952, these strikes, named after the admiral's

Conflicts—Answers

ancestry, were the focus of half the carrier air effort through the end of the war.

86. The **Batfish** (SS-310). Under the command of Cdr. J.K. Fyfe, the **Batfish** sank three Japanese submarines in four days.

87. It was the US Navy's first unequivocal victory over units of the Japanese Navy at night.

88. Three. The USS **Leary** (DD-58) became the third and last on Christmas Eve in 1943.

89. Lt. (jg) Everett Alvarez. He was captured 5 August 1964.

90. The US and South Vietnamese effort to prevent infiltration of men and arms to the South by monitoring, boarding and searching coastal vessels

91. The USS **Juneau** (CL-119) shelled enemy troop concentrations at Okkye.

92. Thirteen. The USS **Callaghan** (DD-792) was the last (28 July 1945).

93. The mining of North Vietnamese harbors 8 May 1972 by aircraft from US carriers in the Gulf of Tonkin

94. 27 January 1973; Paris, France

95. Light Attack Squadron (VAL) FOUR (withdrawn from South Vietnam in April of 197'

Conflicts—Answers

96. Five

97. The surface attack on the Japanese amphibious force at Balikpapan 20 January 1942

98. The destroyer raid on Munda, New Georgia, the night of 4-5 January 1943

99. Adm. W.H. Halsey

100. A small piloted bomb capable of over 500 mph in the terminal dive used by the Japanese against US ships.

101. Enemy air attack accounted for forty-nine.

102. The USS **Ward** (DD-139) sank a Japanese midget submarine shortly after 0630 7 December 1941.

103. Capt. W.S. Parson

104. Rear Adm. Rembrandt C. Robinson, Cruiser-Destroyer Flotilla Eleven. He was killed when his helicopter crashed into the Gulf of Tonkin.

105. Lt. Robert Frishman USN, Capt. Wesley L. Rumble USAF and Seaman Douglas B. Hegdahl USN

106. The US Navy River Patrol Force whose efforts were concentrated on the inland waters of South Vietnam

107. True

Conflicts—Answers

108. None

109. Among other improvements, the Mark 18, a 29-knot torpedo, was electrically driven and left no steam-oxygen bubbles to create a wake.

110. Fletcher

111. The USS **Drayton** (DD-366)

112. The German U-boat **U-58**, sunk by the USS **Fanning** (DD-37) and the USS **Nicholson** (DD-52) in November 1917

113. It was the flag flown by Commodore Matthew C. Perry on his historic voyage to Japan in 1853 (on loan to Admiral Halsey from the US Naval Academy for the occasion).

114. Five; Lt. John F. Kennedy, Lcdrs. Lyndon B. Johnson, Richard M. Nixon and Gerald R. Ford and Midshipman James E. Carter, Jr.

115. Germany

116. Lt. Clyde E. Lassen (assigned to the destroyer **Preble**)

117. Adm. Chester A. Nimitz

118. Twenty-nine

119. "Axis Sally"

120. The sinking of the USS **Maine** 15 February 1898 in Havana Harbor

Conflicts—Answers

121. Thanh Hoa Railroad and Highway Bridge

122. The Japanese submarine **I-173** was sunk by the USS **Gudgeon** (SS-211) (26 January 1942).

123. Over 800

124. The **Wadsworth**, **Conyngham**, **Porter**, **McDougal**, **Davis** and **Wainwright**

125. Eighty-five

126. The USS **Bunker Hill** (CVA-17)

127. They were Army Air Corps B-25 bombers about to launch from the deck of the USS **Hornet** as part of the "Doolittle Raid" on Tokyo in April 1942.

128. The Japanese Heavy Cruiser **Mikuma** at the Battle of Midway

129. The USS **Laffey** (DD45). One of the shortest, most active careers of any naval vessel. Commissioned in March 1942 and sunk at the battle of Savo Island 15 November 1942, she is credited with sinking two destroyers, a cruiser and demolishing the superstructure of a battleship.

PERSONALITIES

1. Who said, "We have met the enemy, and they are ours"?

2. Identify the first pilot to fly from the improvised flight deck of a US Navy ship.

3. Name the ship from which this historic flight was made.

4. Who first landed an aircraft on a ship? What was the name of the ship?

5. Who had the distinction of becoming the first Naval Aviator?

6. Identify the naval officer who became known as the "Father of Naval Aviation."

7. Name the US Navy's first rear admiral.

8. The Navy's first successful catapult aircraft launch was accomplished with what intrepid Naval Aviator at the controls of an AH-3?

33

Personalities—Questions

9. Identify the former assistant secretary of the Navy who became the first US president to submerge in a submarine and fly in an airplane.

10. Identify the Navy's first Naval Aviation Pilot (NAP).

11. Identify the Naval Aviator who at nineteen years of age became the US Navy's only World War I ace.

12. On 7 February 1984 what Naval Aviator became the first human satellite by stepping into space from the space shuttle **Challenger** without being fastened by a line?

13. Identify (in order) five Navy men who succeeded President Eisenhower in that office.

14. What US president was assistant navigation officer and director of physical education during World War II on board the USS **Monterey?**

15. What future US president was awarded the Navy and Marine Corps medal for his actions following the loss of his command to the Japanese destroyer **Amagiri**?

16. Future president Lcdr. Lyndon B. Johnson was onboard the "Heckling Hare" when attacked by Japanese aircraft in the vicinity of New Guinea. What was the "Heckling Hare"?

Personalities—Questions

17. Identify the leading WWII US submarine commander in terms of the number of enemy ships sunk.

18. What Naval Aviator has the distinction of shooting down the most enemy aircraft in one day?

19. Name the only surviving member of Torpedo Squadron Eight at the Battle of Midway.

20. What Naval Aviator was the first US astronaut to make a suborbital flight 5 May 1961?

21. What Naval Aviator, later US senator, became the first US astronaut to orbit the earth 20 February 1962? How many orbits did he make?

22. Name the first US Naval Aviator to qualify as a rotary wing or helicopter pilot on 15 April 1944.

23. Who commanded the Navy NC4 aircraft that made the first successful crossing of the Atlantic Ocean?

24. Who was credited with the following message: "Air raid Pearl Harbor, this is no drill"?

25. Name the first black man designated Naval Aviator.

26. Name the Medal of Honor winner who was the leading World War II US Navy ace. How many victories did he have?

Personalities—Questions

27. Name the Medal of Honor winner who became the US Navy's first World War II ace—downing five aircraft in four minutes.

28. Who was the US Navy's first landing signal officer (LSO)?

29. This noted World War II warrior ran his first command aground on a mudbank in Batangas Harbor in the Philippines and was found guilty of "neglect of duty" by a court-martial. He was later promoted to the rank of lieutenant, skipping lieutenant junior grade, eighteen months after the grounding and went on to become a five star admiral. Name him.

30. On 1 December 1921 the first flight of an airship inflated with helium gas was made at Norfolk, Virginia. Name the pilot.

31. On 21 April 1943 the first jet flight by a US Naval Aviator was completed. Name the aircraft and pilot.

32. What naval officer was the main participant in the Navy's initial live test of an ejection seat?

33. Who said, "We are ready now," in response to the question "When will Destroyer Squadron 8 be ready for service?"

34. Responding to oppressive practices on the high seas and ruinous commerce policies, which US president asked Congress to declare war on Great Britain 1 June 1812?

Personalities—Questions

35. Who was the first naval officer to serve as chairman of the Joint Chiefs of Staff?

36. Name the first six captains appointed in the US Navy.

37. Who was commander in chief of the Pacific Fleet at Pearl Harbor 7 December 1941?

38. Name the American who, never having run a shipyard, organized and directed the construction of over 2,700 Liberty ships throughout the United States between 1941 and 1945.

39. What noted historian and diplomat established the Naval Academy in 1845 while serving as President Polk's secretary of the Navy?

40. "Blood is thicker than water" is attributed to what US naval officer to characterize his intervention in the British attack on the Peitro forts during the Second China War?

41. Who fired the first shell fired by the US Navy in World War I?

42. What noted American commodore resigned his commission in 1826, after twenty-eight years' service, to accept an appointment as commander in chief of the Mexican Navy?

43. A famous World War II admiral held the following philosophy for selecting his subordinate commanders: "every dog

Personalities—Questions

should be allowed two bites"—only after two failures would he replace a commander. Name this gifted judge of professional ability.

44. Commodore Matthew C. Perry's brother Oliver is best known for what event?

45. What famous naval officer was the World War II leader of the "Little Beavers"?

46. Who was the first American in space?

47. Who became the first Navy woman pilot to carrier qualify in a fixed-wing aircraft?

48. Name the Navy's first female aviator who won her wings at NAS Corpus Christi in February of 1974.

49. Who said "The Lord gave us two ends to use: one to think with and one to sit with. The war depends on which we choose—heads we win, tails we lose"?

50. Who is credited with establishing the doctrine and organizing the convoy system of World War I?

51. What colorful World War II figure was nicknamed "Bull"?

52. Serving as the eighth and eleventh superintendent of the US Naval Academy, this officer was the only man ever to hold that position twice. Identify him.

53. Lts. Joseph P. Kennedy, Jr. and Wilford J. Willey were lost during the initial

Personalities—Questions

flight of a World War II special operation code named "Anvil." What was Operation Anvil?

54. Of the first seven men selected as prospective astronauts for Project Mercury, how many were Naval Aviators?

55. Who was the Navy's research pilot in NASA's X-15 program?

56. What famous American naval officer achieved flag rank in the Mexican Navy?

57. What American naval officer is considered the founder of oceanography?

58. What World War II figure was nicknamed "Thirty One Knot"?

59. What naval officer was the first man to reach the North Pole?

60. On 3 March 1915 the Office of the Chief of Naval Operations was established. Name the first naval officer to serve in that position.

61. What US Naval Academy graduate was the first to measure the velocity of light **and** the first American scientist to receive the Nobel Prize?

62. Who was the first Naval Aviator to win the Medal of Honor?

63. Who is the only naval officer to ever hold the rank Admiral of the Navy?

Personalities—Questions

64. Name the young naval officer who, frustrated with slow response from the Bureau of Ordnance concerning improvements and prescriptions for naval gunnery, wrote President Theodore Roosevelt 16 November 1901 to condemn the Navy's gunnery and offer improvements.

65. Who is considered to be the "Father of the Nuclear Navy"?

66. Who was the first Naval Academy graduate to hold the "highest office in the land"?

67. What was the final resting place for John Paul Jones?

68. Name the only Navy ace of the Korean War and the first Navy nightfighter ace.

69. What American admiral ordered his ships to "turn on the lights" to help pilots return to their carriers at night?

70. According to Clay Blair's historical study **Silent Victory**, what US congressman, returning from the war zone in June 1943, provided the following to the news media—who published it: "Don't worry about our submarines; the Japanese are setting their depth charges too shallow"?

71. One of the only two people to ever receive two congressional gold medals was President Zachary Taylor; the other is an American naval officer. Name him.

Personalities—Questions

72. Name the naval officer who, at age forty-nine, became the youngest four-star admiral and the youngest Chief of Naval Operations in the history of the US Navy.

73. Name the former Navy fighter pilot who became the first man to walk on the moon 20 July 1969.

74. Name the first woman line officer to attain flag rank in the US Navy.

75. Name the first woman to earn the badge of a surface warfare officer.

76. Name the first woman to attain flag rank in the US Navy.

77. Name the first black man to attain flag rank in the US Navy.

78. What naval officer is known as the "Father of the Seabees"?

79. What famous American served as the operations officer for the Navy Air Transport Unit on Bougainville, Vella Lavella and finally Geen Island in the South Pacific during World War II?

80. What naval officer is known as the "Father of Modern Naval Ordnance"?

81. What eminent naval officer is credited with converting the Navy to the computer age?

82. Who was the Navy's first master chief?

Personalities—Questions

83. Name the last enlisted Naval Aviator.

84. Whose motto was: "I will find a way or make one"?

85. What naval officer said, "We are not pushed willy-nilly into specialization; there is never an excess of the all-around, highly competent combat officer"?

86. Of seventeen Medals of Honor awarded to the US Armed Forces during World War I, how many were won by officers of the Navy Medical Department serving in the field with Marines?

87. Name the first woman to graduate from the US Naval Test Pilot School in June of 1983.

88. Of the six men who raised the American flag on Mt. Suribachi, Iwo Jima, on 23 February 1945, how many were in the Navy?

89. Who was the first US Navy man to earn the Medal of Honor in Vietnam?

90. What naval officer began his naval career assigned to the Navy physical training unit headed by former boxing champion Gene Tunney?

91. Mildred E. Gillars is better know to World War II servicemen by what name?

92. What US president was the first to transit the Panama Canal?

93. Identify the first woman naval officer.

Personalities—Questions

94. Who was this man?

Personalities—Questions

95. Who is this officer?

Personalities—Questions

96. Who is the officer speaking?

Personalities—Questions

97. Who are these men?

Personalities—Questions

98. Who is this man?

Personalities—Questions

99. Who was this man?

Personalities—Questions

100. Who was this man?

Personalities—Questions

101. Who was this man?

Personalities—Questions

102. Who was this man?

Personalities—Questions

103. Who was this man?

Personalities—Questions

104. Who was this man?

Personalities—Questions

105. Who is this man?

Personalities—Questions

106. Who is this man, and why is he smiling?

Personalities—Questions

107. Who is this man?

Personalities—Questions

108. Who was this man?

Personalities—Questions

109. These midshipmen ultimately became some of our most distinguished naval officers. Who are they?

A

B

C

D

Personalities—Questions

F

H

J

ANSWERS

1. Oliver Hazard Perry, during the Battle of Lake Erie

2. Eugene Ely in a Curtiss biplane

3. The USS **Birmingham**. Ely's aircraft touched the water off Hampton Roads before he was able to level off and fly over two miles—landing on Willoughby Spit near the naval base in Norfolk, Virginia, 14 November 1910.

4. Eugene Ely (17 February 1911); The USS **Pennsylvania** (in San Francisco Bay)

5. Lt. T.G. Ellyson

6. Rear Adm. William A. Moffet

7. D.G. Farragut

8. Lieutenant Ellyson

9. Theodore Roosevelt

Personalities—Answers

10. Harold H. Karr

11. Lt. (jg) David S. Ingalls

12. Capt. Bruce McCandless II

13. Presidents Kennedy, Johnson, Nixon, Ford and Carter

14. Gerald R. Ford

15. Lt. John F. Kennedy, commanding officer aboard the PT-109

16. A B-25

17. Cdr. Richard H. O'Kane, USS **Tang** (SS-306, thirty-one credited during the conflict, twenty-four according to a postwar survey)

18. David McCampbell downed nine Japanese aircraft on 24 October 1944.

19. Ens. George Gay

20. Cdr. Alan Shepard

21. Lt. Col. John Glenn, USMC; Three

22. Lt. W.G. Knapp

23. Lcdr. Albert C. Reed

24. Lt. Patrick Bellinger. Bellinger was also pilot of the first aircraft to sustain combat damage at Vera Cruz. In 1919 Lt. Bellinger and Lcdr. Marc Mitscher crewed the NC1 aircraft that attempted the first transatlantic crossing with NC3 and NC4.

Personalities—Answers

25. Jesse L. Brown. Ensign Brown's F4U Corsair was shot down near the Chosin Reservoir in Korea. Despite heroic rescue attempts by squadron mates, Bown died before he could be freed from the wreckage.

26. Capt. David McCampbell; Thirty-four

27. Lcdr. Edward H. O'Hare

28. Comdr. Kenneth Whiting, the executive officer and senior aviator onboard the USS **Langley**, regularly observed flight operations from the stern and would "coax" aircraft safely aboard with a combination of body English and arm waving. Much to Whiting's surprise, Lieutenant Pride questioned Whiting's signals as to his (Pride's) height above the ramp following a landing. Following a meeting of all **Langley** pilots, it was decided that an experienced pilot should be positioned on the port side aft to signal each landing as per Whiting's call—too high, too low and OK with appropriate manual signals.

29. Chester William Nimitz

30. Lcdr. R.F. Wood

31. **Airacomet** XP-59A; Capt. Frederick M. Trapnell

32. Lt. (jg) A.J. Furtek was ejected from a JD-1 at 250 nautical miles per hour, 6,000 feet over Lakehurst, New Jersey, 30 October 1946. The first emergency

Personalities—Answers

use was made by Lt. J.L. Fruin of Fighter Squadron 171 in August 1949 upon determining that he had transitioned from pilot to passenger in a single seat F2H-1 Banshee at 500 kts over South Carolina.

33. Cdr. J.K. Taussig, USN, commander of the first United States Destroyer Squadron to reach Europe, 1917

34. President James Madison

35. Admiral Arthur W. Radford (1953-1957)

36. Captains Joshua Barney, John Barry, Richard Dale, Samuel Nicholson, Silas Talbot and Thomas Truxtun

37. Adm. H.E. Kimmel

38. Henry Kaiser

39. George Bancroft

40. Commodore Josiah Tattnall (June 1859)

41. J.O. Sabin, the gun pointer onboard the **Jupiter**. The target was an enemy submarine in the Bay of Biscay, 5 June 1917.

42. Commodore David Porter

43. Adm. Chester W. Nimitz, commander of the US Pacific Fleet and the Pacific Ocean Area for World War II

Personalities—Answers

44. While commanding American naval forces on Lake Erie, Commodore O.H. Perry personally led his forces to victory over the British squadron commanded by Cdr. Robert Barclay, RN, in the Battle of Lake Erie 10 September 1813.

45. Arleigh Burke

46. Cdr. Alan B. Shepard traveled 116 miles high and 302 miles down range from Cape Canaveral, Florida, on 5 May 1961.

47. Lt. Donna Spruill landed a C-1A onboard the USS **Independence** 20 June 1979.

48. Lt. (jg) Barbara Ann Allen

49. Adm. C.W. Nimitz (sent as a motto to Admiral Halsey)

50. Adm. William Sowden Sims

51. Fleet Adm. William F. Halsey, Jr.

52. Rear Adm. C.R.P. Rodgers

53. Kennedy and Willey were to have flown a specially modified PB4Y-1 drone filled with explosives to a predetermined point over England and then bail out. The aircraft would then be controlled by a trailing aircraft to a target. Shortly after takeoff from RAF Fersfield, England, on 12 August 1944, the PB4Y exploded over Blythburgh, England.

Personalities—Answers

54. Four (Lt. M.S. Carpenter, Lt. Col. J.H. Glenn, USMC, Lcdr. W.M. Schirra and Lcdr. A.B. Shepard)

55. Cdr. Forrest S. Petersen made five X-15 flights, between 25 August 1958 and 30 January 1962, performing research on problems associated with controlled, manned aircraft flown at extreme altitude and Mach.

56. David Porter

57. Lt. Matthew Fountaine Maury

58. Adm. Arleigh Burke

59. Cdr. Robert E. Peary, Civil Engineer Corps (6 April 1909)

60. Rear Adm. William S. Benson

61. Albert Michelson (Class of 1873)

62. Ensign Charles H. Hammann, USNRF. Ensign Hammann evaded his pursuers during an air-to-air engagement with a superior number of Austrian aircraft on 21 August 1918. He landed his damaged aircraft on the water and rescued a fellow pilot downed in the dogfight.

63. Adm. George Dewey

64. Lt. William S. Sims. Sims, Bradley Fiske and Lcdr. Albert P. Niblack revolutionized gunnery with Roosevelt's support.

Personalities—Answers

65. Adm. Hyman Rickover, USN (Ret.)

66. James E. Carter, Jr. (Class of 1947)

67. The crypt beneath the Naval Academy chapel

68. Lt. G.P. Bordelon. Flying the F-4U5N Corsair, Lieutenant Bordelon downed five North Korean aircraft, all at night, between 29 June and 16 July 1953.

69. Adm. Marc A. Mitscher (following the Battle of the Philippine Sea)

70. Congressman Andrew Jackson May. Vice Adm. C.A. Lockwood, commander of US submarines in the Pacific, wrote: "I consider that indiscretion cost us ten submarines and 800 officers and men."

71. Adm. Hyman G. Rickover

72. Adm. Elmo R. Zumwalt

73. Neil A. Armstrong

74. Rear Adm. Fran McKee

75. Ens. Roberta L. McIntyre

76. Rear Adm. Arlene B. Duerk, Nurse Corps, USN

77. Rear Adm. Samuel L. Gravely, Jr.

78. Adm. B. Moreel

79. Lcdr. Richard M. Nixon

Personalities—Answers

80. Rear Adm. John Adolphus Dahlgren

81. Commodore Grace Hopper

82. Sai Manning—later Cdr. Sai Manning

83. Master Chief R.K. Jones, Naval Aviation Pilot (retired 31 January 1981)

84. Adm. Robert E. Peary

85. Adm. Forrest P. Sherman

86. Three

87. Lt. Colleen Nervius

88. One, Pharmacist's Mate Second Class John H. Bradley. The other five, Sgt. Michael Strank, Cpl. Harlan H. Block and Pfcs. Franklin R. Sousley, Rene A. Gagon and Ira H. Hayes, were all Marines.

89. CM-3 Marvin G. Shields (9 June 1965)

90. Ens. Gerald R. Ford

91. "Axis Sally"

92. Franklin D. Roosevelt aboard the heavy cruiser USS **Houston** (CA-30), 11 July 1934

93. Lt. Mildred Helen McAfee; She was inducted 24 August 1942 to command the WAVES (Women Appointed for Voluntary Emergency Service).

Personalities—Answers

94. Adm. Marc A. Mitscher, Commander of the 8th Fleet, seated in a cockpit of a SB2C.

95. Chester A. Nimitz

96. Admiral Elmo Zumwalt, shown her, as Commander, US Naval Forces, Vietnam. He was later appointed as Chief of Naval Operations.

97. Vice Admiral John S. McCain, USN (left) and Captain Harold M. Martin, USN

98. Admiral William F. Halsey, Jr., USN, Commander Third Fleet

99. Naval aviation pioneer, Rear Admiral W.A. Moffett, USN

100. Fleet Admiral Ernest J. King, USN

101. Rear Admiral Daniel V. Gallery, USN. He commanded the Task Group that captured a German U-Boat (**U-505**) during a surface engagement and also authored several books, including **Eight Bells and All's Well** and **Standby to Start Engines**.

102. Admiral Forrest P. Sherman, Chief of Naval Operations from 2 November 1949 to 22 July 1951

103. Albert Michelson, graduate of the US Naval Academy and the first person to calculate the speed of light

104. Commodore Oliver H. Perry

Personalities—Answers

105. One of the great enlisted naval pilots of World War II, Machinist D.E. Runyon, USN, who is credited with downing eight Japanese aircraft during the month of August 1942

106. Commander David McCampbell, USN, shown in the cockpit of his Grumman "Hellcat." He shot down a record thirty-four enemy aircraft on a single tour of duty.

107. Alan B. Shepard—astronaut, test pilot and naval officer

108. Fleet Admiral W.D. Leahy, USN

109.
   a) W.A. Moffett, pioneer Naval Aviator
   b) William F. Halsey, Commander Third Fleet, World War II
   c) Robert J. Natter, one of the most highly decorated naval officers of the Vietnam War
   d) Marc Mitscher, Commander Eighth Fleet, World War II
   e) John McCain, World War II hero, father of Admiral John McCain, Commander in Chief, Pacific and grandfather of Congressman John McCain, Vietnam POW, Naval Aviator
   f) Arthur MacArthur, son of Gneral Arthur MacArthur. His brother Douglas went to West Point and ultimately acquired his own navy.
   g) Ernest J. King, Fleet Admiral, World War II
   h) Forrest P. Sherman, former Chief of Naval Operations
   i) W.D. Leahy, Fleet Admiral, World War II
   j) Daniel Gallery, pioneer Naval Aviator, author

NAVY LORE

1. Who issued and what prompted the following order: "Damn the torpedoes! Captain Drayton, go ahead! Jouett, full speed!"?

2. Who said, "I wish to have no connection with any ship that does not sail fast, for I intend to go in harm's way"?

3. What famous American naval hero held a commission as rear admiral in the Imperial Russian Navy?

4. What noted American naval officer answered, "I have not yet begun to fight," in response to the hail, "Have you struck?"

5. The dictum "no pilot is any better than his last landing" is associated with what noted grandfather?

6. Name the source of the following familiar opening line: "Eternal Father, strong to save."

Navy Lore—Questions

7. The words, "You may fire when ready, Gridley," were spoken by a naval officer destined to become the only Admiral of the Navy. What was his name?

8. Who said "Fire!"?

9. What country's warships rendered the first salute to the Stars and Stripes at sea? What US ship was involved in this historic first?

10. Name the US Navy's first warship with propelling machinery below the waterline.

11. Identify the US warship described as a "cheesebox on a shingle."

12. On 4 January 1934 the US Navy commissioned the first aircraft carrier to be built as such from the keel up. What was the name of the carrier?

13. Identify the Continental Navy's **last** ship, which was finally sold in June 1785.

14. Following the Civil War, the US Navy was significantly reduced until it consisted mostly of obsolete sloops/gunboats and steam frigates. On 3 March 1883 President Arthur signed a bill to remedy this situation which called for construction of steel-hulled ships. The first four vessels authorized became known as the "ABCD ships." What were the names of these ships?

15. On 18 April 1942 Doolittle's B-25 Tokyo Raiders launched from which US aircraft carrier?

Navy Lore—Questions

16. With which famous carrier is the name "The Fighting Lady" associated?

17. Beginning in 1799, Congress passed a law restricting (and in 1851-1853 further restricted) a shipboard practice that was not abolished entirely until congressional action on 17 July 1862. The Navy Department reported that it would be "utterly impractical to have an efficient Navy without this form of punishment." What was this punishment/practice that was ultimately abolished?

18. Sometimes referred to as "the sailor's disgrace," this symbol is found in various Navy crests (e.g., the cap device of American naval officers and the collar device of the midshipman). What is another name for this symbol?

19. Considered by most seagoing US Navy personnel a dismal day, 1 September 1862 is associated with the abolishment of what daily ritual aboard US Navy ships?

20. Identify the first Navy aircraft carrier with an angled flight deck.

21. What was the first aviation unit trained to operate as a squadron from an aircraft carrier?

22. Identify the US Navy's first fleet ballistic missile submarine.

23. On 22 July 1943 the Vice Chief of Naval Operations approved removal of

Navy Lore—Questions

arresting gear and associated equipment for landing over the bow of aircraft carriers due to the lack of operational need. Some nine years earlier, on 21 June 1934, a US aircraft carrier landed aircraft in the bow arresting gear while the ship went full speed astern. Name the carrier involved.

24. Name the first US jet aircraft to undergo adaptability testing for shipboard operation on board the USS **Franklin D. Roosevelt**?

25. A significant advancement in the development of personal flight equipment was initiated 24 October 1933 with authorization to the Naval Aircraft Factory to produce a special abdominal belt for use in "dive bombing and other violent maneuvers" under the direction of Lcdr. J.R. Poppen, Medical Corps. This early effort was the forerunner of what commonly worn article of personal flight equipment?

26. What was the first US torpedo boat—launched January 1890?

27. The first battleships to mount sixteen-inch guns were of which class?

28. Name the first US battleship to use oil as a source of energy for the engineering plant.

29. Name the first hospital ship, fitted out in 1898, specifically assigned for that purpose.

Navy Lore—Questions

30. What branch of the Navy is referred to as "The Silent Service"?

31. How does a pollywog differ from a shellback?

32. What common requirement exists for membership in the "caterpillar club"?

33. The Venerable Order of the Gray Eagle is a prominent award within naval aviation. Identify the criterion for receiving this award.

34. Who was the US Navy's first director of aviation?

35. What ship had the distinction of being the most decorated ship in the US Navy?

36. What naval officer has been referred to as the "last absolute monarch on earth"?

37. What is the binnacle list?

38. True or False: Prior to the American Civil War there was no rank of admiral in the Navy and no uniformed counterpart to the General-in-Chief of the Army.

39. The flag flying on the USS **Missouri** during the Japanese surrender ceremonies 2 September 1945 was unique for what reason?

40. What is "channel fever"?

Navy Lore—Questions

41. What is unique about the berthing arrangements of the USS **Recruit**?

42. When is the anchor aweigh?

43. When was the Chief Petty Officer (CPO) first included in the ratings?

44. Identify the source and the occasion of the following quote: "There'll always be an England in the United States Navy."

45. What is Rope Yarn Sunday?

46. The WAVES were established by an act of Congress 31 July 1942. For what does the acronym stand?

47. On what date were brown shoes, the traditional footwear in naval aviation, deleted from officer's and chief's uniforms?

48. What is the dog watch?

49. What US Navy combatant, the oldest commissioned ship in the Navy, is known as "Old Ironsides"?

50. What is "Field Day"?

51. What are reef points?

52. What does the term "Dead Horse" mean?

53. What was the first US battleship built after the Washington Naval Conference of 1922?

Navy Lore—Questions

54. What is another name for the North Star?

55. What was the life span of the Continental Navy?

56. Between 1775 and the present, how many years has the United States been without a Navy?

57. When was the first predecessor of the Navy Supply Corps established?

58. What was the first ship of the US Navy to get underway?

59. What was the first victory of the US Navy over an enemy warship?

60. When prescribed, the ship's bell is sounded on the hour and half hour following the motion of the senior officer present, from reveille until taps. Over a four-hour watch, the bells would range from one bell at the end of the first half hour to eight at the end of the four-hour watch. Match the following bells with the corresponding time:
    1) One bell   A. 1500
    2) Two bells   B. 1230
    3) Three bells   C. 0730
    4) Four bells   D. 0930
    5) Five bells   E. 1300
    6) Six bells   F. 1400
    7) Seven bells   G. 2000
    8) Eight bells   H. 1030

61. What is a "Goblin"?

Navy Lore—Questions

62. True or False: Aboard Navy ships, flag hoists are read from the top down, inboard to outboard.

63. Where are you most likely to find the "big eyes" on a Navy ship?

64. What is a Bogey?

65. What were the "Woozlefinches"?

66. Who or what is the COB aboard Navy submarines?

67. What is a Momsen Lung?

68. What part of the enlisted person's uniform has remained unchanged for over a century?

69. What was the first US naval vessel to cross the equator?

70. What is Fiddler's Green?

71. Who or what were Ead's Turtles?

72. True or False: "Stone Fleets," old vessels filled with stones and concrete and sunk by blockading forces at or in harbor entrances in order to seal off harbors, were frequent and effective actions during the Civil War.

73. One of the more colorful graduates of the US Naval Academy became the first American to command a modern battleship in action while serving in the Imperial Chinese Navy. Identify this well-known legend who took over from the

Navy Lore—Questions

captain of the Chen Yuen at the Battle of the Yalu in the Sino-Japanese War.

74. What secretary of the Navy abolished the traditional officer's wine mess aboard naval vessels?

75. Who were the Yeomanettes?

76. What is "sick bay"?

77. What is a "Skunk"?

78. What was the first monument established in the Yard at the US Naval Academy?

79. Who fills the position of president of the wardroom mess aboard US Navy ships?

80. Who introduced coffee to the Navy?

81. Established during World War II, Naval Construction Battalions are more commonly known by what name?

82. What is a "jack-o'-the-dust"?

83. True or False: Juniors always get into a boat ahead of (and leave after) their seniors, unless the senior officer in the boat gives orders to the contrary.

84. What is the Union Jack?

85. What is the only flag ever flown over the national ensign on the same hoist?

Navy Lore—Questions

86. Aboard ship who or what is the "oil king"?

87. For what is an OBA used?

88. What is EMCON?

89. Who is the "featured star" in man-overboard exercises?

90. When were the grades of senior and master chief petty officer established in the US Navy?

91. In 1845 the rum ration on US Navy ships was equivalent to what monetary value on a daily basis?

92. Within naval aviation, the Navy's oldest Naval Flight Officer on active duty is referred to by what term?

93. What was the last rope-making activity in the Navy?

94. Distinguishing marks or specialty marks on rating insignia were prescribed for members of the US Navy in 1841. What was the first adopted?

95. What was the only ship in the Navy with a bathtub?

96. What Navy ship had the first automatic dishwasher?

97. True or False: Instituted in 1852, the officer's boat cloak remains an optional garment for evening wear with any uniform.

Navy Lore—Questions

98. How many stars encircle the eagle on the naval officer's uniform buttons?

99. True or False: Every anchor, except small boat anchors and lightweight type anchors of less than one hundred pounds, has a serial number cast or cut in the crown prior to delivery, when purchased for Navy use. Also included on the opposite side of the crown is the weight in pounds, year made and "US Navy."

100. What former Navy Bureau was known as the "Gun Club"?

101. Who said: "There is a homely adage which runs, 'Speak softly and carry a big stick; you will go far.' If the American nation will speak softly and yet build and keep at a pitch of the highest training a thorough efficient navy, the Monroe Doctrine will go far"?

102. "Hail to the Chief" is designated as a musical tribute to the president of the United States, what is the corresponding selection for the vice president?

103. Who composed "Anchors Aweigh"? When was it composed?

104. What are rainbow sideboys?

105. When did "cracker jacks," the sailor's traditional white hat, jumper and bell-bottomed trousers, give way to double-breasted coats, shirts, ties and caps?

Navy Lore—Questions

106. What is the meaning of the small circle on the port fluke of the anchor in the center of the wings of a Naval Aviator?

107. What US naval combatant was known as the "Galloping Ghost of the Java Coast"?

108. True or False: The United States Navy had no official flag of its own until 24 April 1959 when the flag of the US Navy was created by order of President Eisenhower.

109. What is the name of this vessel?

Navy Lore—Questions

110. What are these men preparing for, and why are they **not** smiling?

ANSWERS

1. David G. Farragut, during the Battle of Mobile Bay, as the US ships entered a minefield 5 August 1864

2. John Paul Jones (in a letter to le Ray de Chaumont, November 1778)

3. John Paul Jones

4. John Paul Jones (in reply to Capt. Richard Pearson, RN, who commanded the ship **Serapis**, off Flamborough Head, 23 September 1775)

5. "Grampaw" Pettibone of **Navair News**

6. It is the first line of the Navy Hymn, "Eternal Father."

7. Adm. George Dewey, at Manila Bay in 1898

8. Captain Gridley, commanding officer, USS **Olympia** (C-G)

9. France; The **Ranger**, John Paul Jones commanding, was saluted by French warships at Quiberon Bay in 1778.

Navy Lore—Answers

10. The **Princeton**

11. The USS **Monitor**

12. The **Ranger**

13. The USS **Alliance**

14. **Atlanta**, **Boston**, **Chicago** and **Dolphin**

15. The USS **Hornet** (CV-8)

16. The USS **Yorktown** (CV-10)

17. Flogging. Although widely supported, groups of sailors presented petitions to Congress requesting no change in the system, stating that without drastic punishment the good men would have to do the work of the shirkers. In December 1862 Secretary of the Navy Guideon Wells reported it was impossible to re-enlist the better class of seamen. This generated a change in the enlistment system and training within the Navy.

18. Foul anchor

19. The spirit ration, "two dips a day and in lieu thereof a commutation of five cents per day," became history when the following words became law: "on September 1, 1862, the spirit ration shall forever cease and therafter no distilled spirituous liquor shall be admitted on board vessels of war..."

20. The USS **Antietam** (CV-36)

Navy Lore—Answers

21. Fighter Squadron 2 which had begun landing practice on the USS **Langley** off the coast of San Diego in January 1925.

22. The USS **George Washington** (SSN 598). Originally designed to be the **Scorpion**, the Navy ordered it to be completed as the first fleet ballistic missile submarine in 1959. The **George Washington** was converted to an attack submarine in 1980 and decommissioned in 1985.

23. The USS **Ranger** (CV-4). Following the completion of normal flight operations, Lcdr. S.C. Davis led the ships' aviators in the "bow on" recovery.

24. The FD-1 Phantom. Lcdr. James Davidson performed takeoffs and landings.

25. Anti-G suit

26. The **Cushing**, named for Lt. W.B. Cushing, who commanded the steam launch that sank the Confederate ironclad **Albemarle** in October 1864.

27. Maryland

28. The USS **Delaware**

29. The USS **Solace**. The concept is credited to Adm. W. Knickerbocker Van Reypen. The 1864 Navy **Register** entry for the **Red Rover** was "Hospital Steamer."

Navy Lore—Answers

30. The submarine force

31. A shellback is a person who has crossed the equator and has been suitably initiated; a pollywog has that once-in-a-lifetime experience to anticipate.

32. The use of an aircraft parachute for its designed purpose

33. This award is held by the oldest Naval Aviator on active duty.

34. Capt. Washington I. Chambers

35. The USS **Franklin**

36. The commanding officer of a navy ship

37. Originally, it was a list placed on the binnacle each morning by the ship's surgeon to indicate to the captain and watch all personnel not available for full duty. Today it is a listing of personnel not fit for full duty but not hospitalized.

38. True

39. The same flag had flown over the US Capitol building the day the Japanese attacked Pearl Harbor 7 December 1941.

40. The overall anticipation/excitement onboard as a ship approaches the end of a deployment and the start of long-awaited liberty. Severity is directly proportional to the length of the deployment and inversely proportional to the distance from homeport.

Navy Lore—Answers

41. The USS **Recruit** is a scaled-down frigate replica permanently berthed in concrete at the Naval Training Center in San Diego, California.

42. When the anchor is no longer in contact with the bottom

43. 1893

44. Signal made by Adm. Ernest J. King, Commander-in-Chief of the United States Fleet, to the destroyer escort USS **England** following her sinking of six Japanese submarines in less than a month off the Admiralty Islands in May-June of 1944.

45. According to the **Origins of Sea Terms** it is "a half-holiday from regular work aboard ships, usually on Wednesdays —but never on Sunday—for the crew to work on their own gear and light odd jobs."

46. Women Accepted for Volunteer Emergency Service

47. 30 June 1976. This occasion was observed with appropriate ceremonies at the officers clubs of many Naval Air Stations.

48. A two-hour watch, 1600-1800 and 1800-2000—a practice that enables the crew to change the times of their watches every day

49. The USS **Constitution**

50. A term used throughout the Navy for a thorough house cleaning.

Navy Lore—Answers

51. Short ropes attached to a sail which are used to shorten sails in heavy weather.

52. A name given to the period of time after a ship's sailing in which her crew was working off advanced wages.

53. The USS **North Carolina** (BB-55), authorized by Congress in 1936

54. Polaris

55. Almost ten years. It was founded 13 October 1775, and the last vessel, **Alliance**, was sold 3 June 1785.

56. Nine (3 June 1785 to 27 March 1794)

57. 23 February 1795—Congress established the Office of Purveyor of Supplies.

58. The USS **Ganges**. Capt. Richard Dale got underway from Philadelphia, 24 May 1798.

59. The USS **Constellation**, commanded by Capt. Thomas Truxtun, defeated and captured the French frigate **L'Insurgente**, commanded by Capt. M.P. Barreaut, on 9 February 1799.

60. 1) B   5) H
    2) E   6) A
    3) D   7) C
    4) F   8) G

61. An unidentified submerged contact assumed to be hostile.

Navy Lore—Answers

62. False. Flag hoists are read top down, outboard to inboard.

63. The signal bridge

64. An unidentified air contact assumed to be hostile.

65. The naval batteries consisting of five fourteen-inch railway guns that provided long range bombardment of German positions during World War I

66. Chief of the boat, the senior chief petty officer aboard a submarine

67. A submarine escape lung. First tested 8 May 1929, the Momsen Lung was developed by Lcdr. C.B. Momsen, Chief Gunner C.L. Tibbals and Mr. Frank Hobson.

68. The petty officer rating badge which has been in use since 1886

69. The USS **Essex**, Capt. Edward Preble commanding, 7 February 1800 enroute to the East Indies

70. A traditional paradise for sailors who die on land—the old name for a seaman's heaven "where the grass is green, fiddlers play, wine flows and mates not permitted."

71. Seven shallow draft ironclad gunboats constructed by James Eads of St. Louis for use on Confederate waterways. As the name implies, the profile of these boats was similar to that of a turtle.

Navy Lore—Answers

72. False. Although used by both sides, Stone Fleets were not effective in closing off and restricting traffic into and out of various harbors.

73. Philo McGiffen (Class of 1882)

74. Josephus Daniels (1 July 1914)

75. During World War I, the Navy was authorized to enlist women to perform yeoman's duties—more than 11,000 women served during World War I.

76. A compartment, cabin or suitable area aboard ship reserved for the treatment of sick/injured sailors.

77. An unidentified surface contact assumed to be hostile.

78. The Mexican Monument. Erected in 1848 by the midshipmen at the Academy, the monument honors four midshipmen who were killed in the Mexican War: H.A. Clemson, J.R. Hynson, J.V. Pillsbury and T.B. Shubrick.

79. The Executive Officer

80. Chaplain Jones. On 10 February 1842 Jones wrote to the secretary of the Navy offering to buy coffee if the Navy "would furnish conveniences for having it prepared."

81. Seabees

82. An appointee of the supply officer who assists in issuing stores and cleaning storerooms

Navy Lore—Answers

83. True

84. A flag flown by ships at anchor from 0800 to sunset. It is a replica of the blue, star-studded field of the national ensign.

85. The church pennant. The church pennant is displayed only during services conducted by a chaplain.

86. The petty officer who maintains records of fuel oil, makes tank soundings and provides assistance when the ship takes on fuel

87. As an oxygen breathing apparatus. The OBA protects the wearer from gases, vapor, smoke or an atmosphere lacking oxygen.

88. Emission control—the positive management of electromagnetic emissions at various levels ranging from all systems emitting to a complete shut down of all emitters

89. A buoyant dummy named "Oscar"

90. 1958 (to provide additional recognition to individuals with outstanding technical, leadership and supervisory abilities)

91. Five cents

92. The Gray Owl

93. The ropewalk at the Boston Naval Shipyard was closed 31 December

Navy Lore—Answers

1971 after 147 years of operation. From this point onwards, the Navy's rope has been made by private firms.

94. Boatswain's Mate (two anchors with long stems and flukes, crossed, and foul with rope)

95. The USS **Iowa** (BB-61). The bathtub was part of the special "cruise gear" installed for President Franklin D. Roosevelt.

96. The USS **Missouri** (BB-11). The dishwasher was introduced by Paymaster George P. Dyer in 1904. Dyer later added the first automatic potato peeler, ice cream mixer and meat slicer.

97. True

98. Thirteen

99. True

100. The Bureau of Ordnance

101. Theodore Roosevelt (at the Minnesota State Fair, 2 September 1901)

102. "Hail Columbia"

103. Lt. Charles A. Zimmerman, the Naval Academy bandmaster, and Midshipman Alfred H. Miles in a joint effort in 1907. It was first sung by midshipmen at the Army/Navy football game in 1907—a game that Navy won.

Navy Lore—Answers

104. Customary sideboy honors aboard an operating aircraft carrier performed by flight deck crewmen wearing their normal colored jerseys.

105. 1 July 1973

106. It is called a "becket." In Navy terminology a becket is an eye for securing one end of a line to a block. Anchors used on sailing ships had a becket on one of the flukes to which a line was attached to secure it to the side of the ship, to keep it from moving when the ship was underway.

107. The USS **Houston**

108. True

109. The USS **Maine**, of "Remember the **Maine**" fame

110. Seabag inspection, 1933 vintage. No one ever smiles during a seabag inspection—not even in 1933.

HISTORY

1. What were Yankee and Dixie Stations?

2. What Navy aircraft set the record for the longest production run for any US military aircraft?

3. What was the US Navy's first Talos missile cruiser?

4. The illegal seizure of an American merchant ship by a Cambodian gunboat in international waters on 12 May 1975 prompted the US president to authorize a rescue. US Air Force helicopters with 288 Marines from Battalion Landing Teams 2 and 9, with protective air strikes from the USS **Coral Sea**, achieved the release of the ship and crew. Name the merchant ship and US president involved.

5. Operation Homecoming was the name given to the repatriation of US prisoners of war (POW) between 27 January and 1 April 1973. Of 591 POWs released, how many were Navy personnel?

History—Questions

6. The world's first guided missile cruiser was placed in commission at the Philadelphia Naval Shipyard. Name the ship.

7. What was the first operationally equipped jet aircraft to fly faster than 1,000 miles per hour?

8. Who took the oath of office 17 September 1947 as the first secretary of defense?

9. What was the first carrier-qualified jet squadron in the US Navy?

10. What Navy aircraft was known as the "Yellow Peril"?

11. What was the device known as "Glomb"?

12. What was the first operational unit of the US Navy to be supplied with radar-equipped aircraft?

13. True or False: The US Navy placed two converted aircraft carriers on the inland waters of Lake Michigan into service in 1942 and operated them there through the end of the war.

14. When did the Navy accept its first helicopter?

15. Who made the first night carrier landing?

History—Questions

16. On 9 May 1926 the first flight over the North Pole was accomplished. Identify the two Naval Aviators involved.

17. Who is credited with the following: "Whosoever commands the sea commands the trade; whosoever commands the trade of the world commands the riches of the world, and consequently the world itself"?

18. What was the total number of North Vietnamese MiG aircraft shot down by Navy and Marine aircrews during the Vietnam conflict?

19. Name the first submarine built from the keel up with guided missile capability.

20. What world famous aviation unit, organized and led by Lcdr. R.M. Voris, completed its first airshow over Jacksonville, Florida, in June 1946?

21. What was the first Navy jet fighter to fly simultaneously with the Navy, Marine Corps and Air Force and the only fighter ever to fly concurrently with the Navy's Blue Angels and the Air Force Thunderbirds?

22. Casualties from the Battle of Manila Bay were as follows: Spain—167 sailors killed, 214 wounded; the United States—one fatality, eight wounded. What caused the one US fatality?

23. What was an "E-Boat" during World War II?

History—Questions

24. What is the oldest type of ship to see continuous service in the US Navy?

25. In the words of Theodore Roosevelt, the tragic event of 7 May 1915 was "piracy on a vaster scale than the worst pirates of history." 1,198 people, including 124 Americans, were killed. What was this tragedy that influenced America to enter World War I?

26. True or False: No United States battleship was ever lost at sea in action with the enemy.

27. Identify the only Navy ship named in honor of a woman.

28. What was the first American destroyer?

29. What was Mulberry Harbor in World War II?

30. If you were involved with logistics during the Allied effort against Germany in Europe, you would know that "Pluto" was not just a cartoon character. What else was "Pluto"?

31. Who commanded the Great White Fleet during the around-the-world cruise of 1908-9?

32. What vessel led the Great White Fleet out of Hampton Roads 9 December 1908 as it began its the around-the-world cruise?

History—Questions

33. What was the last major combat ship lost by the United States in World War II?

34. Where and when was the peace treaty between America and Great Britain which officially ended the Revolutionary War signed?

35. What was the Quasi-War with France?

36. What was the first British warship defeated in the War of 1812?

37. True or False: Along with Britain, Italy and Japan, the United States made extensive use of midget submarines during the Second World War.

38. Who was selected as the first Master Chief Petty Officer of the Navy (MCPON)?

39. Eight days after the United States and Great Britain formally concluded the War of 1812, President Madison requested Congress to declare war against what foreign power in response to renewed attacks on American merchant shipping?

40. Who claimed the Oregon Territory for the United States on 19 August 1818?

41. What was the first naval engagement in the War with Tripoli?

42. Who were known as "Preble's Boys"?

History—Questions

43. Called by Britain's Lord Nelson "the most daring act of the age," one of Preble's Boys led a group of eighty volunteers into Tripoli Harbor, boarded the captured frigate **Philadelphia**, overcame the guards, set fire to the ship and escaped with one man injured. Name this naval officer who was promoted to captain for his actions and at twenty-five years of age was (and remains) the youngest man ever to attain that rank.

44. Responding to oppressive practices on the high seas and ruinous commerce policies, which US president asked Congress to declare war on Great Britain 1 June 1812?

45. How many US battleships were in commission at the start of the Korean War in 1950?

46. What is the common link between the Chesapeake-Leopard Affair, Commodore James Barron and Commodore Stephen Decatur?

47. True or False: On 21 December 1861 Congress created the Navy Medal of Honor to reward petty officers, seamen and marines "as shall most distinguish themselves by their gallantry in action and other seamanlike qualities." The Army Medal of Honor followed in July 1862.

48. The first amphibious operation of the Civil War occurred 28-29 August 1861 when US forces captured what strategic location?

History—Questions

49. What was the Anaconda Plan which the United States followed during the Civil War?

50. Who was the first US Navy officer killed in the American Civil War?

51. What is the US Navy's first experience with aeronautics?

52. Laying of the first Atlantic cable was completed 5 August 1858. The cable enabled the first transatlantic message to be sent from Queen Victoria to President James Buchanan. What US vessel was involved in this historic achievement?

53. What was the first US naval vessel to visit China?

54. The West Indies Squadron was founded in 1822 for what purpose?

55. What famous US combatant is known as "Mighty Mo"?

56. What was the Shimonoseki Incident?

57. Who became the US Navy's first vice admiral?

58. During the course of the American Civil War, approximately how many US ships were sunk or damaged by Confederate mines?

59. When was the Civil Engineering Corps established?

History—Questions

60. What was America's first overseas territory?

61. Name the US Naval Academy's first Japanese graduate.

62. Congress authorized the Navy Good Conduct Medal in April 1869. The present bronze medal was adopted in 1892. What was the shape of the original award?

63. The Navy Department ordered construction of the first torpedo station in 1869 at what location?

64. Who was the US Navy's first surgeon-general?

65. True or False: The Office of Naval Intelligence (ONI) was established in 1930.

66. Authorized for construction by Congress 6 August 1886, name the US Navy's first two battleships.

67. What provoked the Chilean Crisis of 1892?

68. What was the first US naval vessel armed with torpedoes?

69. What was the first steam-powered American naval vessel to sail around the world in 1880?

70. Name the first naval attache assigned to the London embassy in 1882 to report on technological developments in European navies.

History—Questions

71. The first five bureaus in the Navy's bureau administrative organization were established in 1842. Name them.

72. True or False: The side-wheel frigate **Missouri**, commanded by Capt. John T. Newton, was the first steam-powered US Navy vessel to cross the Atlantic in 1843.

73. Who was responsible for annexing America's first overseas territory, Nukahiva Island in the Marquesas, to the United States 19 November 1813?

74. What significant event in April 1814 on the Continent enabled the British to focus more of their attention and resources to their ongoing efforts against America?

75. The Treaty of Ghent signed at Ghent, Belgium, on Christmas Eve and ratified by Congress two months later ended what war?

76. What was the source of the following message: "Underway on nuclear power"?

77. Name the second nuclear-powered submarine in the US Navy.

78. Where was the US Navy's first dry dock located?

79. What conflict was the largest Indian war fought by the United States east of the Mississippi and the only one in which the US Navy played a significant role?

History—Questions

80. Who was the first engineer to be commissioned in the US Navy?

81. How could you determine whether a Naval Aviator was a balloon pilot or in the Lighter-than-Air-Service?

82. When was the Navy Nurse Corps established?

83. Authorized by Congress 3 June 1898, name the first official American campaign medal.

84. True or False: The steamer **Michigan** was the US Navy's first iron-hulled vessel.

85. How many Mexican naval vessels broke the US Navy blockade during the Mexican War?

86. Six years before Commodore Perry's first visit to Japan the first two American warships anchored in Tokyo Bay in an unsuccessful attempt to open diplomatic relations with Japan. Name the ships involved.

87. America's first real scientific institute, the Nautical Almanac Office, was established at _____ on 3 March 1849.

88. What was the Flying Squadron, formed in March 1898?

89. During World War I NOTS was established to control the shipment of supplies to American forces in Europe. For what did NOTS stand?

History—Questions

90. What was the US Navy's first armored cruiser?

91. Name the first US strategic missile to be deployed.

92. What was the first and the only US submarine to successfully launch the Regulus II missile?

93. Name the US Navy's **only** two-reactor submarine.

94. In response to the attack on Pearl Harbor, what noted American naval officer offered the following opinion: "The way to victory is long/The going will be hard/We will do the best we can with what we've got/We must have more planes and ships—at once/Then it will be our turn to strike/We will win through—in time"?

95. What was the first US naval vessel to travel through the newly opened Panama Canal in October 1914?

96. What two Naval Aviators made the first night "hook-ons" to the trapeze suspended from the airship USS **Los Angeles** on 29 September 1931?

97. What was the last rigid airship built and flown in the United States?

98. Founded in March of 1900, what was the purpose of the General Board of the Navy? Who served as its first president?

99. When was the US Navy's first destroyer commissioned?

History—Questions

100. The first take off from a US aircraft carrier occurred 17 October 1922. Name the pilot.

101. On 18 November 1922 the first catapult launch from a US carrier was made. Name the pilot.

102. Who was the first pilot to land on an American carrier while underway?

103. How many units opened the year after the Naval Reserve Officer Training Corps (NROTC) was established by Congress in 1925?

104. Women midshipmen were admitted to the Naval Academy in what year?

105. Renamed the Bureau of Personnel in 1942, what was the original title?

106. Who introduced the practice of numbering US fleets?

107. Name three significant decisions of major importance to the Navy resulting from the first Washington Conference (Arcadia) between President Roosevelt and Prime Minister Churchill in early 1942.

108. What was the only US Navy rigid airship that did not meet a violent end?

109. Who was the first COMYANGPAT or "Commander of the Yangtze Patrol"?

110. As a result of the Washington Naval Treaty of 1922, the US, Great Britain,

History—Questions

Japan, France and Italy concluded the Five-Power Treaty of naval arms limitations and established what ratio for capital ships?

111. Under the London Naval Treaty of 1930, the US, Great Britain and Japan established what ratio for cruiser tonnage?

112. What was the Potsdam Declaration?

113. Name the first US submarine to launch a missile.

114. Name the US combatant that made the first successful launch of a V-2 ballistic missile.

115. What was the first peacetime military alliance the US entered?

116. What Chief of Naval Operations was relieved, primarily for his testimony to the House Naval Affairs Committee, in what became known as the Revolt of the Admirals?

117. What are structures aboard ship which combine masts and stacks called?

118. What was the name of the Navy's first satellite, weighing 3¼ pounds, which was launched from Cape Canaveral, Florida?

119. What was the first ship to sail from the Pacific to the Atlantic by way of the North Pole?

History—Questions

120. What was the first submarine to surface at the North Pole?

121. What was the Navy's first navigational satellite?

122. What US submarine was the first to launch the Polaris A-1 missile while submerged?

123. What was the world's first nuclear-powered, guided-missile cruiser?

124. What was the Navy's first hydrofoil patrol craft?

125. What was the Navy's first nuclear-powered, guided-missile frigate?

126. What was the Navy's primary role in the Cuban missile crisis of October 1962?

127. What was the first of the supercarriers?

128. Where was the Navy's first nuclear power school established?

129. The US Naval Academy first included women among the graduates of what class?

130. What was the Gulf of Sidra Incident in 1981?

131. What submarine made the last Polaris missile patrol?

132. Name the mission commander for Operation Urgent Fury—the US landing on the Caribbean island of Grenada 25 October 1983.

History—Questions

133. Closed in 1974, this shipyard facility had been the Navy's oldest. What was its name?

134. The first submerged launch of the Poseidon missile was made from which SSBN?

135. Name the US technical research ship that was repeatedly attacked by Israeli aircraft and torpedo boats while operating in international waters north of the Sinai Peninsula in June 1967.

136. Name the US intelligence collection ship captured by North Korean patrol boats in international waters 22 January 1968.

137. What was the name of the first two-man Gemini space capsule to orbit the earth?

138. What was the first fleet ballistic-missile submarine to make a patrol in the Pacific?

139. Identify the first American submarine to be designated as a "fleet" submarine.

140. What were the first US submarines to have a stern torpedo tube?

141. True or False: No US submarine has been modified to carry a fixed wing aircraft.

142. The largest submarine constructed by the United States prior to World War II was designed and built for what specific purpose?

History—Questions

143. The crew of what US submarine was the first to enjoy air conditioning?

144. What was the purpose of the snorkel on submarines?

145. Name four innovations incorporated in various US aircraft carriers that were adapted from the British.

146. What was the first commissioned Trident submarine?

147. What was the first destroyer to serve as plane guard?

148. What was the first of the US post-Washington Naval Treaty heavy cruisers?

149. Identify the first secretary of the US Navy, who was nominated by President John Adams.

150. Identify the world's first steam-powered warship.

151. Converted from the collier **Jupiter**, the Navy's first aircraft carrier was commissioned 20 March 1922. What was the name of this historic ship?

152. Departing from NAS Rockaway Beach, New York, the first transatlantic flight was accomplished eight years before the nonstop solo flight of Charles Lindbergh by what Navy aircraft?

153. What was the first all-jet Navy aircraft?

History—Questions

154. Who or what was the "Truculent Turtle"?

155. What was the US Navy's first ironclad vessel named?

156. "Remember the Maine!" is a slogan from which US conflict?

157. Name the last traditional naval battle fought with no intervention from aircraft or submarines, with the fleet advancing into battle in the traditional line ahead and with the enemy using the tactic of crossing a 'T'.

158. Where was the USS **Maine** sunk?

159. What was the first ship to reach the geographic north pole and the first ship to complete a voyage across the top of the world?

160. Who was the Continental Navy's Commander in Chief of the Fleet?

161. Name the first nuclear submarine.

162. Name the US Navy's first submarine.

163. Name the US Navy's first dreadnaught.

164. Name the first US warship to circumnavigate the world.

165. Name the first submarine to circumnavigate the world while submerged.

History—Questions

166. What was the name of the first American-built ship of the line? Who commissioned it?

167. Where did Naval Aviator #1 undergo his flight instruction?

168. What US aircraft carrier launched the first aircraft by a hangar deck catapult on 7 November 1938?

169. How many aircraft carriers did Japan lose during World War II?

170. Who said of the US submarine effort in the World War II, "We shall never forget that it was our submarines that held the lines against the enemy while our fleets replaced losses and repaired wounds"?

171. Name the first ship of the US Navy equipped to carry and operate aircraft.

172. Who was the second American to land on an American ship—this time the USS **Langley** (CU-1) underway off Cape Henry?

173. Who described one of the Navy's early personnel challenges in the following way: "When the **Trenton**, our best ship, lately went into commission, as fine a body of Germans, Huns, Norsemen, Gauls, Chinese, and other outside barbarians as one could wish, softened down by time and civilization, were on board. Out of the whole crew not more than eighty could speak the English language"?

History—Questions

174. Who abolished the Navy's traditional practice of enlisting Filipinos to serve as mess stewards?

175. Who was the first black graduate of the US Naval Academy?

176. Regulations promulgated in 1870 expressly forbid the use of steam. For many years ship's captains were required to make log entries stating their reasons for getting up steam in what color ink?

177. Name the oldest artificial satellite orbiting the earth.

178. What was the last Navy FRAM destroyer on the active ship's list?

179. Name the first class of destroyers to use cafeteria-style messing rather than the berthing style system where mess cooks carried trays to tables set up in the crew's compartment for each meal.

180. The United States Coast Guard operated under the Navy for what period of time during World War II?

181. According to Adm. William S. Sims, what constituted a fast carrier?

182. Charles Lindbergh flew the **Spirit of St. Louis** from New York to Paris nonstop—how did he get back?

183. What assistant secretary of the Navy ordered that all midshipmen and recruits

History—Questions

learn to swim before they joined the fleet after he discovered that invariably more men died from drowning than injuries when a ship sunk?

184. Who was the first member of the House of Representatives to enter active duty in World War II?

185. Nicknamed the "Yankee Racehorse" by French sailors, name the oldest ship of the Navy.

186. Name the first cruiser since World War II designed and built as such from the keel up.

187. What was the Navy's lead ship in the first class of patrol hydrofoil missile ships?

188. What is the purpose of the Navy's Phalanx close-in weapon system?

189. What was the last US combat aircraft to launch from an aircraft carrier without the use of a catapult?

190. How many Navy and Marine Corps enlisted pilots were there between 1920 and 1981?

191. A UCLA graduate with a degree in zoology, Mrs. Iva Toguri d'Aquino is better known by what name?

192. Who was William Joyce?

History—Questions

193. What was the sponsor who brought the world the "Greater East Asia Co-Prosperity Sphere"?

194. In 1916 Congress voted funds for the creation of a laboratory to be devoted entirely to naval research as a result of the persuasive arguments of what noted chairman of the Naval Consulting Board?

195. What was the first US Navy combat vessel equipped with a bow thruster to assist in maneuvering?

196. When was the first significant replenishment operation performed at sea, and what ships were involved?

197. What state was the first to use a source of reserve naval manpower in 1888 when it organized a naval battalion as part of the state militia?

198. What was the first US Navy combatant equipped with anti-aircraft missiles?

199. On 22 June 1973 the **Skylab I** astronaut team operating the world's first orbiting space laboratory completed a thirty-day operation. What did the members of the team all have in common?

200. What Fletcher class destroyer was named by order of President Franklin D. Roosevelt in honor of five brothers from Iowa who were killed in the cruiser **Juneau** at the Battle of Guadalcanal during November of 1942?

History—Questions

201. The US Navy first used HUK groups in 1943—what were they?

202. Where was the first naval hospital constructed?

203. Approximately how many spectators were on hand when the Navy's first iron-hulled warship, the **Michigan**, was launched the evening of 5-6 December 1843?

204. Name the first US Navy ship named for an enlisted man.

205. What event which happened the evening of 8 September 1923 was considered "the biggest single peacetime accident to befall any navy"?

History—Questions

206. "Well, Senator, it seemed like a good idea at the time..." What is it?

History—Questions

207. What is the designation of this aircraft?

History—Questions

208. What is the name of this vessel?

History—Questions

209. What are these aircraft, and what is the carrier?

History—Questions

210. What is the name of this vessel?

History—Questions

211. What is this aircraft?

History—Questions

212. Describe this event.

History—Questions

213. What is this aircraft?

History—Questions

214. What is the name of this vessel?

History—Questions

215. What are these men celebrating?

History—Questions

216. Who are these men, and what is significant about them?

History—Questions

217. What is the significance of this landing, and what are the aircraft and ship involved?

History—Questions

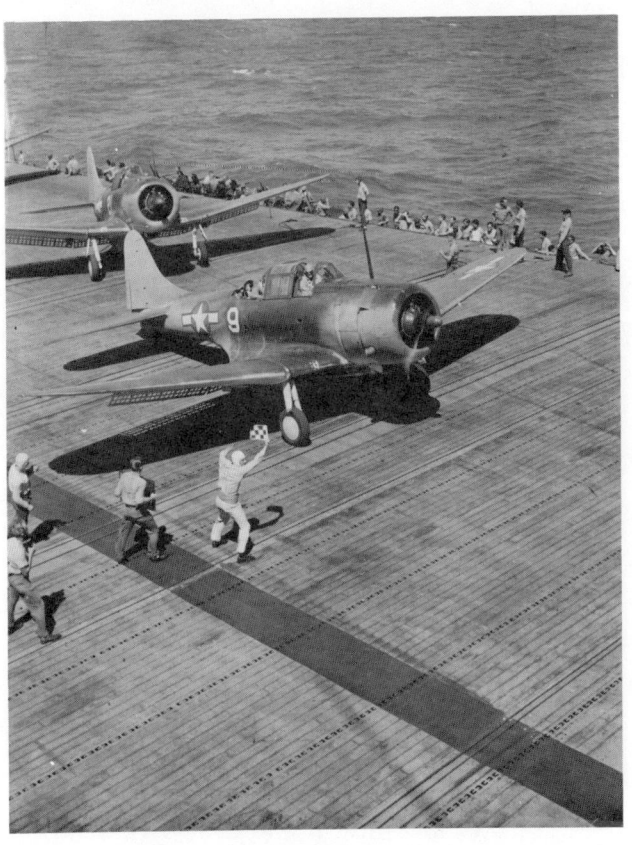

218. What aircraft is this?

History—Questions

219. What is the name of this vessel?

History—Questions

220. "Are you nuts? You want me to **fly** this thing?" What is it?

History—Questions

221. Who were these men?

History — Questions

222. What is the significance of this event?

History—Questions

223. What is the name of this vessel?

History—Questions

224. What is the name of this vessel?

History—Questions

225. What is this aircraft?

ANSWERS

1. Operating locations for US aircraft carriers off the coast of North and South Vietnam

2. The A-4 Skyhawk. On 27 February 1979 the US Navy took delivery of the last A-4 after twenty-six years of its continuous production.

3. The USS **Galveston** (CLG-3), commissioned 28 May 1958

4. The USS **Mayaguez;** President Gerald Ford

5. 145

6. The USS **Boston** (CAG-1)

7. The F-8U Crusader, piloted by Cdr. R.W. Windsor, established a new national speed record of 1,015.4 mph over a fifteen-kilometer course at China Lake, California, 21 August 1956.

8. James Forrestal, Secretary of the Navy

History—Answers

9. Fighter Squadron 17-A qualified all squadron pilots (and the Air Wing Commander!) with a minimum of eight takeoffs and landings in three days of operations aboard the USS **Saipan** (CVL-48).

10. N3N-1, a primary trainer biplane

11. A glider "bomb" designed to be towed long distances, released and guided by radio control to the target.

12. Patrol Wing 7 (mid-September 1941)

13. True, the USS **Wolverine** and the USS **Sable** were two converted Great Lake excursion ships that were used to train student Naval Aviators as well as flight deck crews.

14. October 1943. Lcdr. F.A. Erickson, USCG, performed the acceptance flight for the Sikorsky YR-4B (HNS-1).

15. Lt. John D. Price, VF-1, made the first night landing on the USS **Langley** at sea off San Diego. Price was followed by Lieutenants D.L. Conley, A.W. Gorton and R.D. Lyon 8 April 1925. Earlier, on 5 February, Lieutenant H.J. Brow's accidental landing occured when he stalled while making night practice approaches.

16. Lcdr. R.E. Byrd and Aviation Pilot Floyd Bennet (on 29 November 1929 Lcdr. Byrd flew over the South Pole

History—Answers

and dropped, from a trap door in the plane, an American flag weighted with a stone brought from the grave of Floyd Bennet.)

17. Sir Walter Raleigh, **History of the World, 1616**

18. Fifty-seven

19. The USS **Grayback**

20. The Blue Angels

21. F-4 Phantom II

22. A "coal heaver" died of a heart attack.

23. The British and American name for Schnellboot, a German motor torpedo boat.

24. The destroyer

25. The sinking of the RMS **Lusitania** by a German submarine

26. True

27. The USS **Higbee**, in honor of Mrs. Lena Sutcliffe Higbee, the second Superintendent of the Navy Nurse Corps

28. The USS **Farragut**, a 273-ton ship constructed in 1898

29. The artificial, prefabricated harbor constructed off the coast of Normandy in 1944 to supply the Allied invasion of France.

History—Answers

30. The code name for the pipeline under the ocean which joined Southampton and Cherbourg. It provided a continuous supply of petroleum to the Allies.

31. Rear Adm. "Fighting Bob" Evans and Rear Adm. C.S. Sperry

32. The presidential yacht **Mayflower**, with President Theodore Roosevelt onboard

33. The cruiser USS **Indianapolis**, sunk by a Japanese submarine 29 July 1945

34. 3 September 1783; Paris, France

35. An undeclared war between the United States and France, the genesis of which lay in the French harassment of American merchant shipping. On 28 May 1798 Congress directed US warships "to capture any French vessel found near the coast preying upon American commerce."

36. The British sloop **Alert**. Capt. Thomas L.P. Laugharne was defeated in a brief battle (lasting less than ten minutes) by the US frigate **Essex**, commanded by Capt. David Porter, 13 August 1812.

37. False. The US neither built nor operated midget submarines during World War II.

38. Master Chief Gunner's Mate Delbert Black was selected as the first Senior Enlisted Advisor of the Navy. In 1967 Black's title was changed to Master Chief Petty Officer of the Navy.

History—Answers

39. Algiers. The dey of Algiers, unhappy with tribute being paid to him, expelled the US consul, captured the US brig **Edwin** and enslaved the crew.

40. Capt. James Biddle of the sloop **Ontario**

41. The USS **Enterprise**, Lt. Andrew Sterrett commanding, captured the **Tripoli**, off Malta.

42. The commanding officers of the ships in the Third American Mediterranean Squadron. Commanded by Commodore Edward Preble during the War with Tripoli, they became known as "Preble's Boys" because all were less than thirty years of age.

43. Stephen Decatur

44. President James Madison

45. One, the USS **Missouri** (BB-63)

46. Despite a close friendship with Barron, Decatur was ordered to sit on the court-martial board that determined Barron guilty of negligence in the Chesapeake-Leopard Affair. Following the War of 1812, questions as to Barron's character were raised for having spent the entire war in Europe. Believing that Decatur was among those questioning his courage, Barron challenged Decatur to a duel. On the duelling site at Bladensburg, Maryland, in March of 1820, Barron and Decatur all but reconciled their differences and neither shot to

History—Answers

kill. Barron received a wound in the thigh. Decatur, age forty, died an agonizing death twelve hours later from a shot deflected into his groin. Barron recovered to become the senior officer in the Navy, but was never given command at sea.

47. True

48. Forts Hatteras and Clark, which controlled access to the Hatteras Inlet

49. The complete blockade of the Confederate coast and powerful movement down the Mississippi so as to envelop the Southern states

50. Cdr. James H. Ward, first Commandant of Mishipmen at the US Naval Academy, was fatally wounded during an engagement at Mathias Point, Virginia, 27 June 1861.

51. John La Mountain observed the Confederate batteries at Sewell's Point, Virginia, in a captive balloon from the US steamer **Fanny**.

52. The steam frigate **Niagra**, under the command of Capt. William L. Hudson

53. The frigate **Congress**, commanded by Capt. J.D. Henley, left Hampton Roads, Virginia, 16 May 1820 and arrived in December of the same year.

54. To protect American merchant shipping and to suppress piracy off the coast of

History—Answers

Cuba, Puerto Rico and Central America. The first squadron commander was Commodore James Biddle.

55. The USS **Missouri** (BB-63)

56. On 16 July 1863, in response to the attack on the American merchant steamer **Pembroke** in Shimonoseki Strait by ships belonging to Prince Nagata, Capt. David McDougal, in the screw sloop **Wyoming**, entered the straits, sank all three of the prince's warships present and shelled the forts ashore.

57. Rear Adm. David Glasgow Farragut (23 December 1864)

58. Over forty

59. 3 March 1871

60. Midway Island. The US claimed this Pacific island on 28 December 1867. Captain William Reynolds of the sloop **Lackawanna** had raised the flag on 28 August.

61. Midshipman Jiunzo Matsumura (Class of 1873). He will attain the rank of Vice Admiral in the Imperial Japanese Navy.

62. A Maltese Cross (made of nickel)

63. Goat Island at Newport, Rhode Island

64. William M. Wood

65. False. ONI was established in March 1882.

History—Answers

66. The **Maine** and the **Texas**. Although the **Maine** was originally designated "armored cruiser," the **Texas** was an "armored battleship" from the beginning. The battleship **Texas** was the first to be commissioned (15 August 1895); **Maine** was the second (17 September 1895).

67. The True Blue Saloon Incident of 16 October 1891, in which two US sailors from the cruiser **Baltimore** were killed and sixteen injured when the liberty party became involved with a mob of Chileans at the saloon. Rude, offensive remarks by the Chilean foreign minister prompted an ultimatum from President Benjamin Harrison. Chile apologized and payed an indemnity of $75,000 to the families of the two slain sailors.

68. The screw steamer **Intrepid**, commissioned at Boston in 1874

69. The **Ticonderoga**, under the command of Commodore Robert W. Shufeldt

70. Lt. French Ensor Chadwick

71. Yards and Docks; Construction and Repair; Provisions and Clothing; Ordnance and Hydrography; and Medicine and Surgery

72. True

73. Capt. David Porter of the **Essex**. After becoming informed of this months after the fact, the US government ignored Porter's initiative.

History—Answers

74. The defeat and abdication of Napoleon

75. The War of 1812. The US and Great Britain agreed to a pre-war status quo.

76. The USS **Nautilus** (SSN-571)—shortly after 1100 17 January 1955 during her first sea trial

77. The USS **Seawolf** (SSN-575)

78. Charlestown Navy Yard in Boston. The first ship-of-the-line to enter was the **Delaware.**

79. The Second Seminole War

80. Charles H. Haswell. Haswell designed the engines for the second steamship built for the Navy, the **Fulton II**.

81. If the wings were identical to those of a Naval Aviator, except that the wing to the wearer's right was removed, the wearer was a balloon pilot.

82. 13 May 1908

83. The medal awarded for the officers and men who participated in the Battle of Manila Bay.

84. True. The **Michigan** was launched 5 December 1843 at Erie, Pennsylvania, to patrol the Great Lakes.

85. None

86. The **Columbus** and the **Vincennes**, under the command of Commodore James Biddle

History—Answers

87. Harvard University

88. Prompted by the prospect of war with Spain, the Flying Squadron, under the command of Acting Commodore Winfield Scott Schley, was formed for the defense of the East Coast. The following ships constituted the Flying Squadron: armored cruiser **Brooklyn** (ACR-3); battleships **Massachusetts** (BB-2) and **Texas**; cruisers **Columbia** (C-12) and **Minneapolis** (C-13).

89. Naval Overseas Transportation Service. Of more than 450 cargo ships assigned to this service, a total of eight would be lost to enemy action.

90. The **New York** (ACR-2), commissioned 1 August 1893 at Philadelphia

91. The Regulus I was deployed on board submarines and surface combatants until the advent of Polaris in large numbers.

92. The USS **Grayback** (SSG-574) launched one of the eleven-ton Regulus II missiles on 16 September 1958. Regulus II was a short-lived program halted just three months after its inaugural launch in favor of the shift to the Polaris ballistic missile program.

93. The USS **Triton** (SSRN-586)

94. Adm. Ernest J. King, Chief of Naval Operations, December 1941

History—Answers

95. The collier **Jupiter**

96. Lts. Daniel W. Harrigan and Howard L. Young

97. ZRS-5, the dirgible **Macon**. Loss of the Macon off Point Sur, California, 12 February 1935 ended the Navy's operation of rigid airships.

98. The General Board was a permanent board of senior officers who provided the secretary of the Navy with professional advice on naval operations and policy; Adm. George Dewey

99. 24 November 1902 (the torpedo boat destroyer **Bainbridge**)

100. Lcdr. Virgil C. Griffin took off from the flight deck of the USS **Langley** (CV1) in a Vought VE-75F

101. Cdr. Kenneth Whiting, in a PT seaplane. The ship was at anchor in the York River.

102. Lcdr. Godfrey deC. Chavalier landed onboard the **Langley** off Cape Henry in an Aeromarine 39B on 26 October 1922.

103. Six

104. July 1976

105. Bureau of Navigation

106. Adm. E.J. King (15 March 1943)

History—Answers

107. The "Germany first policy" was reaffirmed, the US assumed responsibility for the war in the Pacific and the agreement was made for an Anglo-American invasion of French North Africa in 1942.

108. The dirigible **Los Angeles** (ZR-3) was decommissioned at NAS Lakehurst 30 June 1932.

109. Capt. T.A. Kearney. American gunboats operating on China's Yangtze River for the preceding seventeen years were organized under Capt. Kearney Christmas Day 1919.

110. 5:5:3:1 3/4: 1 3/4 respectively

111. 10:10:7 respectively

112. A statement issued by the Big Three—Truman, Churchill and Stalin—at Potsdam, Germany, calling on Japan to surrender or face "utter destruction."

113. The USS **Cusk** (SS-348). The missile was the Loon, an American version of the German V-1.

114. The USS **Midway** (then CVB-41)

115. The North Atlantic Treaty Organization (4 April 1949)

116. Adm. L.E. Denfeld, the eleventh Chief of Naval Operations, was relieved by Secretary of the Navy Matthews, with the approval of President Truman, 1 November 1949.

History—Answers

117. Macks

118. Vanguard 1 (launched 17 March 1958)

119. The USS **Nautilus** (SSN-571), under the command of Cdr. W.R. Anderson (August 1958)

120. The USS **Skate** (SSN-578), under the command of Cdr. J.F. Calvert (11 August 1958)

121. The Transit IB (launched 13 April 1960)

122. The USS **George Washington** (SSBN-598, 20 July 1960)

123. The USS **Long Beach** (CBN-9)

124. The USS **Long Point** (PC(H)-1)

125. The USS **Bainbridge** (DLGN-25)

126. Naval quarantine

127. The USS **Forrestal** (CVA-59)

128. The submarine base in New London, Connecticut (10 January 1956)

129. Class of 1980

130. Two Libyan SU-22 aircraft attacked and were shot down by two F-14 fighters from the USS **Nimitz** (CVN-68).

131. The USS **Robert E. Lee** (SSBN-601)

132. Vice Adm. Joseph Metcalf III

History—Answers

133. The Boston Naval Shipyard. It had been in operation for 174 years.

134. The USS **James Madison** (SSBN-627)

135. The **Liberty** (AGTR-5)

136. The USS **Pueblo** (AGER-2)

137. **Molly Brown**

138. The USS **Daniel Boone** (SSBN-629, 26 December 1964)

139. The USS **Schley** (SS-52)

140. The post-World War I S-boats (S-10 through S-13)

141. False. The S-1 (SS-105) was fitted to carry and launch an MS-1 floatplane.

142. Laying mines

143. The USS **Cuttlefish** (SS-171)

144. It was essentially a breathing tube which enabled air to be drawn down for diesel engine operation at periscope depth. The snorkel enabled the submarine to charge batteries and significantly reduced the probability of detection as only the snorkel head was above the water.

145. Angled flight deck, hurricane bow, steam catapults and the mirror landing system

History—Answers

146. The USS **Ohio** (SSBN-726)

147. The USS **Roe** served as plane guard for Eugene Ely's first launch from the USS **Birmingham** on 14 November 1910.

148. The USS **Pensacola**

149. Benjamin Stoddert

150. The **Demologos** (Fulton I), designed by Robert Fulton for harbor defense, and armed with thirty-two cannon. The warship, which was propelled by a central paddle wheel, was launched 29 October 1814.

151. The USS **Langley**

152. NC-4 (May 1919)

153. The McDonnell FD-1 Phantom (It was later redesignated the FH-1.)

154. The Navy Lockheed P2V, which flew nonstop and unrefueled from Perth, Australia, 29 September 1946 to Columbus, Ohio, setting a world distance record of 11,235.6 miles in fifty-five hours and seventeen minutes

155. The **Monitor**

156. The Spanish American War

157. The Battle of Surigao Straits, 24 October 1944

158. Havanna Harbor, Cuba, 15 February 1898

History—Answers

159. The USS **Nautilus**

160. Commodore Esek Hopkins

161. The USS **Nautilus** (SSN-571, commissioned 30 September 1954)

162. The USS **Holland**

163. The USS **Michigan** (BB-27)—commissioned January 1910, it was the first to use superimposed turrets which enabled all eight of the ships twelve-inch guns to be trained to either side.

164. The USS **Vincennes**

165. The USS **Triton** (SSRN-586); **Triton** followed closely the route of Ferdinand Magellan in 1529.

166. The **America**, commisioned by John Paul Jones in 1779

167. The Glen Curtis Aviation Camp, North Island, San Diego, California

168. The USS **Yorktown**

169. Twenty

170. Adm. Chester W. Nimitz

171. The USS **North Carolina**. On 12 July 1916 Lieutenant G. deC. Cevalier was catapulted from the **North Carolina** while underway in Pensacola Bay. This event signaled the completion of **North Carolina**'s catapult calibration, and her readiness to carry and operate aircraft.

History—Answers

172. Lcdr. Geoffrey Chevalier, Naval Aviator #7 (26 October 1922), eleven years after Eugene Ely the first landing

173. Adm. David Dixson Porter (1888)

174. Adm. E. Zumwalt (February 1971)

175. Ens. Wesley A. Brown, USN (Class of 1949)

176. Red

177. **Vanguard I**—the second artificial satellite placed in orbit by the US. The Naval Reasearch Laboratory developed the launch vehicle and satellite. Four months prior to the successful launch, Project Vanguard was transferred from the Navy to the National Aeronautics and Space Administration.

178. The USS **Agerholm** (DD-826)

179. The Fletcher class of 1940

180. November 1941 through 1 January 1946 (It then returned to the Treasury Department.)

181. An aircraft carrier capable of thirty-five knots and carrying one hundred planes

182. President Calvin Coolidge dispatched the cruiser **Memphis** to return Lindbergh and his aircraft back to the United States.

183. Assistant Secretary of the Navy Franklin D. Roosevelt

184. Lcdr. Lyndon B. Johnson, USNR

History—Answers

185. The US frigate **Constellation,** the oldest US warship afloat. **Constellation** never lost a battle and was the first American-designed and American-built warship to win a major victory over an enemy man-of-war.

186. The USS **Long Beach** (CGN-9)

187. The USS **Pegasus** (PHM-1)

188. Phalanx is a twenty-mm vulcan gun and fire control system capable of engaging anti-ship cruise missiles that penetrate outer layers of defense.

189. A-1 Skyraider or SPAD, the last piston-engine fighter or attack aircraft to be flown from US carriers

190. 3,700

191. "Tokyo Rose." After the war she was convicted as a traitor, imprisoned and fined. She was finally pardoned by President Gerald Ford in January of 1977.

192. "Lord Haw-Haw." Widely known for his Nazi propaganda broadcasts, Joyce was found guilty of high treason and executed at Wandworth Prison in January of 1946.

193. Japan. This euphemism was attached to the new Japanese Empire of World War II in which everyone would work for the common goal of "Asia for Asians."

194. Thomas A. Edison. The Naval Research Laboratory was completed in 1923.

History—Answers

195. The USS **Newport County** (LST-1179)

196. In 1899 the Navy collier **Marcellus** transferred coal while towing the USS **Massachusetts**.

197. Massachusetts

198. The USS **Gyatt** (DD-712—recommissioned as DDG-1, 3 December 1954)

199. They were all Naval Aviators.

200. The USS **The Sullivans** (DD-537)

201. HUK, Hunter-Killer Groups, consisted of an anti-submarine warfare carrier and a screen of about four destroyers or destroyer escorts; these groups combined the air and surface prosecution of ASW operations.

202. Portsmouth, Virginia (work began 2 April 1827.)

203. None

204. The USS **Osmond Ingram** (DD-255). Ingram was the first enlisted man killed when the USS **Cassin** (DD-43) was torpedoed during October of 1917.

205. Seven ships of Desron Eleven ran aground and were lost off the California coast while carrying out a twenty-four hour test run from San Francisco to San Diego.

History—Answers

206. XF2Y-1 "Sea Dart"

207. F-2-H, "Banshee"

208. The USS **Connecticut** (BB-18)—steaming at high speed in 1907

209. A flight of three F9-F "Panthers" flying over the USS **Boxer** (CV-21) during the Korean War

210. The USS **Utah** (BB-31)

211. A Grumman "Avenger"

212. The USS **Nautilus** (SSN-571) entering New York Harbor after her transpolar voyage under the arctic ice cap

213. XF2A-2 "Brewster"

214. The USS **Yorktown** (CV-5)—after being torpedoed at the Battle of Midway

215. A smashing 17-0 victory over Japanese Zeroes in the Marshall Islands. Lt. (jg) Eugene R. Hanks became an ace in less than five minutes during his encounter with the enemy.

216. The men of Torpedo Squadron Eight. Ens. George H. Gay, kneeling fourth from the left, was the sole survivor of thirty pilots and crew at the Battle of Midway.

217. It is the first "carrier" (ship) landing aboard the USS **Pennsylvania** (ACR4) in San Fransisco Bay. The aircraft,

History—Answers

flown by Eugene Ely, is the Curtiss "Pusher" (note the sophisticated arresting gear).

218. The Douglas "Dauntless" dive-bomber

219. The USS **Thresher** (SS N 593)

220. Convair XFYI vertical takeoff Delta Wing. Don't worry, the Navy decided not to buy the idea!

221. Rear Admiral R.E. Byrd (left) of the 1947 Antarctica Developments Projects and Secretary of the Navy James V. Forrestal shown in conversation with an unknown third party.

222. The first carrier landing of an F4U-4 Corsair

223. The USS **Bunker Hill** (CV-17)

224. The USS **Wyoming** (BB-32)—shown leaving San Diego in 1937

225. A Boeing F4B-S (1933)

GENERAL

1. The Argentine ship **General Belgrano** sunk during the Falkland crisis by a British submarine in May of 1982 was a former US warship which had been present at Pearl Harbor 7 December 1941. What was its name as a US ship?

2. What was the first supersonic, carrier-based aircraft?

3. What 2 September 1944 event became known as "Halsey's Whimsy"?

4. Name the location of the Navy's first permanent air station.

5. What tragic 1919 event provided the motivation for Glenn Curtis to devise the first aircraft seat belt?

6. Name the famous general who made the following observation: "Of all careers, the Navy is the one which offers the most frequent opportunities to junior officers to act on their own."

General—Questions

7. Identify the early historian to whom the enduring quote, "A collision at sea can ruin your entire day," is attributed.

8. True or False: Following the first aircraft landing on a ship 18 January 1911 in a Curtiss pusher, the second landing on a naval vessel occurred within days.

9. What was the Navy's first aircraft?

10. Since 1845, Annapolis, Maryland, has been the site of the US Naval Academy for all but four years of its existence. Identify the "other" location of the Academy.

11. What made the above change of location necessary?

12. The US Navy lost one ship to enemy gunfire on D-Day. Identify the ship.

13. What naval officer is credited with overcoming Japan's isolationism?

14. The first Army-Navy football game was played in what year? What was the final score?

15. How many battleships were included in the Great White Fleet that sailed around the world from 1907-1909?

16. Identify the first US military unit to arrive in France during World War I.

17. On 1 July 1921 five basic ratings were established in the Aviation Branch that

General—Questions

were concerned specifically with aviation and were based solely on aviation requirements. Name the ratings involved.

18. What US Navy airship was the US Navy's first airship, the first American-built rigid airship, the first airship to use helium as a lifting agent, the first to use a water recovery apparatus for the continuous production of ballast from engine exhaust gases and finally, the first rigid airship to fly across the United States?

19. What was the first and only rigid airship to land on an aircraft carrier?

20. What was the first air-to-air missile delivered to carrier squadrons in 1956?

21. What form of naval warfare, dormant in the Navy since the Civil War, was given new life in the Mekong Delta of South Viet Nam in the 1960s?

22. Which Navy aircraft remained in service as a first line combat aircraft longer than any other fighter?

23. NATOPS is an acronym for the aviator's flight "bible." What is the complete title for this often used reference, and when was it adopted for use in the Navy?

24. Identify the naval officer born at West Point who (1) authored **The Influence of Seapower Upon History, 1660-1783**, (2) was among the best known

naval officers of his day, (3) became the second president of the Naval War College and (4) was the recipient of the following unfavorable endorsement to a fitness report rendered in 1893, "It is not the business of a Naval officer to write books."

25. What famous general and later head of state made the following statement: "Yr Excellency will have observed that whatever efforts are made by the Land Armies, the Navy must have the casting vote in the present contest"?

26. The term RADAR was authorized by the Chief of Naval Operations on 18 November 1940 as an abbreviation for what phrase?

27. Although the first appointment of an engineer in the US Navy was in 1836, the corps was not incorporated in the United States Navy **Register** nor organized until what year?

28. What US naval combatant provided electrical power to a West Coast city for thirty days?

29. In 1946 the Aeronautical Board unanimously agreed that the _____ and the _____ be adopted by the Army Air Forces and the Navy as standard units of speed and distance.

30. Name four naval officers who attained the rank of fleet admiral (five stars).

General—Questions

31. In March 1932 Army Air Corps observers witnessed performance trials against the target ship **Pittsburgh** of an improved design for the MK XV sight. What is the name of this Navy-developed sight that became essential to high altitude precision bombing in World War II?

32. What famous submariner made the following observation: "A ship is always referred to as she because it costs so much to keep her in paint and powder"?

33. Who was the first Commander in Chief of the Army and Navy to hold religious services for Navy personnel?

34. Who said, "He who commands the sea has command of everything"?

35. Where is the US Naval Test Pilot School located?

36. TACAN is the acronym for what term?

37. What is an "Irish pennant"?

38. Who made the following prediction: "Of all the tools the Navy will employ to control the seas in any future war . . . the destroyer will be sure to be there"?

39. For what does the acronym SONAR stand?

40. Who was the Greek goddess of navigation?

General—Questions

41. True or False: A lubber's line is a temporary line or lashing extending from a vessel to a pier.

42. How do a hangfire and a misfire differ?

43. What individual aboard ship is often referred to as "sky pilot"?

44. True or False: No United States man-of-war has ever mutinied or been in the hands of mutineers, while in other navies whole squadrons and fleets have mutinied.

45. The Navy Postgraduate School now located in Monterey, California, was first established at another location 1 October 1909. Name the original location.

46. What was Operation Sea Orbit?

47. Where was the physical location of "Battleship Row"?

48. GUPPY is an acronym for what submarine-related expression?

49. What was the largest single class of ships ever built?

50. How many World War II German U-boats are located in the United States?

51. Commodore Matthew C. Perry's first visit to Japan in 1852 was accomplished with two steam frigates. Name them.

52. The US Navy's annual scientific exploration of Antarctica is known by what name?

General—Questions

53. Who described aircraft carriers in the following manner: "An aircraft carrier is a noble thing. It lacks almost everything that seems to denote nobility, yet deep nobility is there. A carrier has no poise. It has no grace. It is top-heavy and lop-sided. It has the lines of a cow. It doesn't cut through the water like a cruiser, knifing romantically along . . . It just plows . . . Yet a carrier is a ferocious thing, and out of its heritage of action has grown its nobility. I believe that every Navy in the world has as its No. 1 priority the destruction of enemy carriers. That's a precarious honor, but it's a proud one"?

54. What is the origin of the term U-boat?

55. One used a "Very Pistol" for what purpose?

56. What is the publication entitled the "International Regulations for Preventing Collisions at Sea" commonly called?

57. Name the first American warship to round Cape Horn.

58. The Bureau of Medicine and Surgery was organized in 1842 by a physician who served as the first Chief and Senior Surgeon of the Navy. Name this individual.

59. If you were attending the Navy's Senior Enlisted Academy, in what part of the country would you now be located?

General—Questions

60. What is the unique qualification for all members of the Navy parachute teams "Chuting Stars" and "Leap Frogs"?

61. For what purpose is the Beaufort Scale used?

62. For what does the acronym FRAM stand?

63. What is the international radiotelephone distress signal?

64. Who was the first Chief of Naval Operations to take the oath of office at a location other than Washington, D.C.?

65. Where is the Navy Supply Corps School located?

66. True or False: The lawyers of the Navy were formed into the Judge Advocate General Corps (JAG Corps) in 1968.

67. Match the color of the flight deck jersey worn by personnel working on the flight deck to the specific task performed:
    1. Aircraft directors/ spotters
    2. Catapult crew
    3. Crash crew
    4. Plane handling crew; chockmen
    5. Plane captain
    6. Fueling crew
    7. Hospital corpsman

    a) Purple
    b) Yellow
    c) Green
    d) Blue
    e) White with red cross
    f) Brown
    g) Red

68. What is the difference between deperming and degaussing a ship?

General—Questions

69. The continent of Antarctica was discovered by what American naval officer?

70. The Pay Corps established by Act of Congress on 3 March 1871 was renamed in 1919. What do we now call the former Pay Corps?

71. With the creation of the Navy's special warfare community in January of 1962, SEAL Teams 1 and 2 were established on the West and East Coasts. For what does the acronym SEAL stand?

72. The Naval Justice School is located where?

73. What is an NEC code?

74. All recruits begin their Navy careers at one of three Naval Training Centers (NTC). Where are they located?

75. All Navy women recruits begin their careers at which Naval Training Center?

76. What is the difference between ratings and rates?

77. Naval officers may be in one of a total of _____ staff corps.

78. Rating badges, worn on the left sleeve of the enlisted person's uniform, are commonly referred to by what term?

79. What is the correct title for the chief petty officer with three stars equally spaced above the eagle on his rating badge?

General—Questions

80. Service stripes, also known as "hash marks," are worn on the left sleeve and below the rating badge. Each strip represents how many years of service?

81. What members of the US Navy wear the gold rating badge and gold service stripes on their blue uniforms?

82. Name the official residence of the Chief of Naval Operations.

83. For what does the acronym CAP stand?

84. What is a SAM?

85. Identify the location of the Naval Observatory?

86. The Far East can be defined as waters east of the _____ Ocean.

87. The United States in World War II built more _____ class destroyers than any other.

88. What is the difference between flotsam and jetsam, if any?

89. What are the names given to the two complete and interchangeable crews of fleet ballistic missile submarines?

90. Name the location of the Navy's first Trident Submarine Base.

91. True or False: Gun salutes, as detailed by Navy Regulations, are fired at intervals of five seconds, and always in even numbers.

General—Questions

92. What is the first general order for a sentry on duty?

93. True or False: A good rule to follow when maneuvering a ship is to turn toward the formation in executing maneuvers whenever possible.

94. What is the title of a vice admiral's counterpart in the US Army, Air Force and Marine Corps?

95. After what are US battleships named?

96. After what are tank landing ships (LSTs) named?

97. After what are fleet ballistic missile submarines named?

98. Ships in the "Gator" Navy are primarily involved with what mission?

99. UNREP is the acronym for what essential evolution for fleet effectiveness?

100. What commissioning source for junior officers for was established under the Holloway Plan?

101. Name the former command that is now known as the Sixth Fleet.

102. On US Navy ships built after March of 1949 the compartment number contains what four elements?

103. The Ohio class submarines carry how many Trident missiles?

General—Questions

104. Name the Navy's first amphibious assault ship.

105. True or False: Similar to aviators, who are awarded wings after graduating from flight school, a graduate of the submarine school at New London received his dolphin insignia upon completion of the course.

106. Prior to nuclear submarines, what facility built more submarines for the US Navy than any other facility?

107. Well-known to the crews of destroyers and submarines, what were "Ashcans"?

108. The civilian version of the Navy's premier land-based patrol aircraft, the P-3 Orion, is known by what name?

109. Since 1977 US attack submarines have been armed with what anti-ship missile?

110. Name the only United States strategic weapon approved for deployment during the decade of the 1970s.

111. US Navy operations with deep submergence vehicles began in 1957 with a chartered bathyscaph. Name the bathyscaph completed in the Italian seaport of the same name in 1953.

112. Name the US Navy's first oil-fired destroyer.

113. The CSS **Alabama**, the most successful commerce raider of all time, was sunk

General—Questions

by what US combatant in a one-sided engagement off Cherbourg, France?

114. During World War II destroyers could create smoke to conceal the movements of friendly units in what two ways?

115. Responsible for training aerospace medical personnel for duty with aviation units throughout the Navy and Marine Corps, the Naval Aerospace Medical Institute is located in _____, _____.

116. What constitutes the main deck of a ship?

117. Where is the Civil Engineering Corps Officer School located?

118. A Navy enlisted person below the pay grade of E-4 wearing red group rate marks on the left sleeve is in what occupational group?

119. Associated with the Fleet Rehabilitation and Modernization Program—what was DASH?

120. Where is the United States Naval Institute located?

121. Identify the Navy's first Aegis cruiser?

122. What is the weight of the Mark II anchor used aboard the supercarriers?

123. What is VERTREP?

124. Which is longer—a statute mile or a nautical mile?

General—Questions

125. What does the acronym STANAVFORLANT represent?

126. What is the nation's oldest personal military decoration?

127. Where is the Naval Amphibious School located?

128. Where are the "Gunsmiths of the Navy" located?

129. What is an AOC? Where might you find one?

130. What is the shortest time in which a modern oceangoing vessel has been built?

131. What is a SLCM?

132. What is SINS?

133. Identify the three major components of the Trident weapons system.

134. What is MAD gear?

135. What was the last fleet ballistic missile submarine authorized?

136. The four destroyers of the Kidd class were originally ordered for what country?

137. What is the nickname for the Kidd class destroyers?

138. What US combatant, now a memorial, was nicknamed the "Showboat"?

General—Questions

139. Where is the Naval Academy Preparatory School (NAPS) located?

140. What are traffic rules aboard ship during general quarters?

141. What term is used to refer to nonjudicial punishment in the Navy?

142. Aboard Navy ships who is the president of the wardroom mess?

143. What is the "Navy Annex"?

144. Explosive Ordnance Disposal (EOD) units are all volunteers who have graduated from the EOD school at what location?

145. The long demanding road to becoming a fully qualified SEAL begins with Basic Underwater Demolition/SEAL (BUDS) at what location?

146. When was the Office of Naval Intelligence established on a "permanent, appropriated basis" by the Congress?

147. Where is the Naval Safety Center located?

148. What has replaced the destroyer as the single most effective antisubmarine platform?

149. What is cavitation?

150. What two variables are recorded when the navigator "shoots" a star with a sextant?

General—Questions

151. The Navy's ships and service craft are officially classified as one of four major categories. Name the categories.

152. Page nine of the Navy Enlisted Service Record contains what kind of information?

153. Cruisers were originally grouped and designated as CLs, CAs and CBs according to what criterion?

154. What is SAR?

155. Where is Topgun, the US Navy Fighter Weapons School, located?

156. What US Navy combatant is referred to as the "Big E"?

157. If you were looking at a sign which read "Welcome to _____ the Annapolis of the Air," where would you be located?

158. Officer and enlisted personnel selected to attend the submarine school do so at what location?

159. What was the US Navy's all-gas turbine warship?

160. What was the first ship to undergo a FRAM I overhaul?

161. Prior to 1838 a naval officer holding the present day rank of commander was referred to by what term?

162. What is LAMPS?

163. Name the first American warship to be named for a foreign city.

General—Questions

164. Name these two carriers.

General—Questions

165. Identify this aircraft and the weapon on the starboard wing station.

General—Questions

166. Identify these aircraft.

General—Questions

167. Identify this aircraft.

168. What is the hole to the left of the taxi light?

169. What is a "HUKKER"?

General—Questions

170. Identify the aircraft.

171. What is the squadron?

172. What is the weapon being fired? (Hint: it is not a sonobuoy!)

General—Questions

173. What is the man on the right doing?

General—Questions

174. What is the name of this vessel?

General—Questions

175. What is the name of this vessel?

General—Questions

176. What is this aircraft, and what is the significance of the flag painted on the tail?

General—Questions

177. What is the name of this vessel?

General—Questions

178. What is the name of this vessel?

187

General—Questions

179. What are these aircraft, and what was their mission?

ANSWERS

1. The **USS Phoenix** (CL-46). It was sold to Argentina in 1951.

2. The F-8 Crusader

3. Following the Japanese surrender, some 1,200 carrier based air and Army Air Force aircraft performed a flyover of Tokyo Bay and the ships present on what can only be considered a grand scale.

4. NAS Pensacola, Florida

5. Pilot Ensign W. Billingsley, Naval Aviator #9, and passenger John H. Towers, Naval Aviator #3, were both thrown from their aircraft when they encountered turbulence over the Chesapeake Bay at 1,600 feet. Towers managed to grab a strut and entered the water with the aircraft. Billingsley fell to his death and was the first Naval Aviator killed in a flying accident.

6. Napoleon Bonaparte (**Political Aphorisms**, 1848)

General—Answers

7. Thucydides (fifth century B.C.)

8. False. Although described by the commanding officer of the **Pennsylvania** as "the most important landing of a bird since the dove flew back to the ark," and by headlines like "Eugene Ely Revises Naval Tactics" in the **San Francisco Examiner**, a decade and World War I would pass before another aircraft would land onboard a US naval vessel.

9. The A-1 Triad, ordered from Curtis, and costing $5,500

10. Newport, Rhode Island

11. The Civil War

12. The USS **Corry** was sunk by gunfire from enemy batteries on Utah Beach.

13. Commodore Matthew Perry

14. 1890; Navy won 24-0.

15. Sixteen

16. The First Aeronautic Detachment, consisting of seven officers and 122 enlisted men and commanded by Lt. Kenneth Whiting, arrived in Pauillac and St. Nazaire, France, aboard the USS **Jupiter** and the USS **Neptune** on 5 and 8 June 1917.

17. Aviation Machinist's Mate, Aviation Metalsmith, Aviation Carpenter's Mate, Aviation Rigger and Photographer

General—Answers

18. ZR-1, **Shenandoah**, completed at NAS Lakehurst, New Jersey, in 1921

19. ZR-3, **Los Angeles**, landed onboard the **USS Saratoga** (1928). **Los Angeles** was also the first airship to conduct aircraft hook-on and launching tests for the US Navy.

20. Sparrow I was the first air-to-air missile provided to US combat units.

21. Riverine warfare

22. F4U Corsair

23. Naval Air Training and Operations Procedures Standardization; 1961

24. Alfred Thayer Mahan

25. George Washington (in a letter to the Comte de Grasse, 28 October 1781)

26. Radio Detection and Ranging Equipment

27. 1843

28. The USS **Lexington** (CV-2). It provided electricity for the city of Tacoma, Washington, from mid-December 1929 to 16 January 1930 as a result of the failure of the city's power supply.

29. Knot, nautical mile

30. William D. Leahy, Ernest J. King, Chester W. Nimitz and William F. Halsey

General—Answers

31. The Norden bombsight

32. Adm. C.W. Nimitz (13 February 1940)

33. President Franklin D. Roosevelt. On Easter Sunday, 1 April 1934, the president, in the absence of a chaplain, stood on the quarter-deck of the **Nourmahal** and read the service from the **Episcopal Book of Common Prayer**.

34. Themistocles (514-449 B.C.)

35. NAS Patuxent River, Maryland

36. Tactical Air Navigation System

37. An unseamanlike, dangling loose end of a line or piece of clothing

38. Adm. C.W. Nimitz (1962)

39. Sound Navigation and Ranging (underwater echo ranging equipment, originally for detecting submarines)

40. Minerva

41. False. A lubber's line is a line drawn on the inside of the bowl of the compass to correspond with the ship's head. The point on the compass card coinciding with this line gives the heading of the ship or the course being steered.

42. A hangfire is a shot that fails to go off on the first attempt to fire, but goes off later. A misfire is a shot which fails to fire.

General—Answers

43. The chaplain (a.k.a. "padre")

44. True

45. Annapolis, Maryland

46. A 65 day and 30,216 nm circumnavigation of the globe by the world's first nuclear-powered task force, the USS **Enterprise**, the USS **Long Beach** and the USS **Bainbridge**—without taking on fuel or provisions.

47. Off the southeast shore of Ford Island and across the main channel from the Navy Yard

48. Greater Underwater Propulsive Power (an effort to enhance underwater performance of the US Navy's fleet subs)

49. Liberty ships. 2,751 were built during President F.D. Roosevelt's emergency World War II shipbuilding program. First of the line was the SS **Patrick Henry**.

50. One. **U-505**, which was boarded and captured in 1944, is now located on the east side of the Chicago Museum of Science and Industry, Chicago, Illinois.

51. The **Mississippi** and the **Susquehana**

52. Operation Deep Freeze

53. War correspondent Ernie Pyle (1945)

54. The German word "unterseeboot," which translated into English means under-sea boat

193

General—Answers

55. As a signal device. It is a pistol named after its inventor Samuel W. Very, a naval officer, from which cartridges containing colored flares can be fired.

56. International Rules of the Road

57. The frigate **Essex** (commanded by Capt. David Porter)

58. Dr. W.P.C. Barton

59. New England, specifically Newport, Rhode Island

60. All members are "on loan" from a SEAL team.

61. To express wind force on a scale of 0 (calm) to 12 (hurricane). The scale was devised by Adm. Beaufort, RN, in 1808.

62. Fleet Rehabilitation and Modernization program—designed to add years to the useful life of the ship

63. MAYDAY (thought to originate from the French **m'aidez**, meaning help me)

64. Rear Adm. Arleigh A. Burke relieved Admiral R.B. Carney at Dahlgren Hall, US Naval Academy, on 17 August 1955. The original ceremony was to have been held onboard the USS **Ticonderoga** but was cancelled because of a hurricane.

65. Athens, Georgia

General—Answers

66. True

67. 1b, 2c, 3g, 4d, 5f, 6a, 7e

68. Degaussing is the method used to **reduce** a ship's magnetism by energizing the degaussing coils with direct current. Deperming is the actual neutralization or stabilization of a ship's magnetic field.

69. Lt. Charles Wilkes. He discovered Antarctica in the sloop **Vincennes** 19 January 1849, one day prior to sightings of the continent by d'Urville's French expedition. Wilkes' observations, the subject of much controversy, were confirmed by Sir Ernest Shackleton in 1908 and 1909.

70. The Supply Corps

71. Sea, Air, Land Team. The SEALS are select personnel highly trained and equipped for unconventional warfare and counter-guerilla and clandestine operations in maritime and riverine areas of the world.

72. Newport, Rhode Island

73. A Navy Enlisted Classification code. NECs reflect specific billets, and personnel qualified by training or experience to fill them. An individual may have up to five NECs, although the primary and secondary are the two most important.

74. Great Lakes, Illinois; San Diego, California; and Orlando, Florida

General—Answers

75. NTC Orlando, Florida

76. Ratings are occupational fields or areas of specialization; rates denote the level within a rating E-1 through E-9.

77. Eight (Medical, Supply, Chaplain, Civil Engineer, Judge Advocate General's, Dental, Medical Service or Nurse)

78. Crows

79. Master Chief Petty Officer of the Navy

80. Four years of active or reserve duty (or a combination thereof) in any of the armed forces

81. Petty officers with a total of twelve years active duty in the Navy or Naval Reserve who have earned successive awards of the Navy Good Conduct Medal

82. Tingey House, Quarters A, Washington Navy Yard

83. Combat Air Patrol

84. Surface to Air Missile

85. Washington, DC

86. Indian

87. Fletcher. 175 destroyers of this class were built during the war.

88. Flotsam is any part of the wreckage of a ship or her cargo found floating on the

General—Answers

sea. Jetsam is goods or equipment which are deliberately thrown overboard and implies abandonment.

89. Blue and Gold. Two crews allow FBM subs to spend the majority of their time at sea by breaking up the long at-sea periods between the two crews.

90. Bangor, Washington

91. False. Salutes are always odd in number (e.g. 21—heads of state, 17—admiral, 15—vice admiral and 13—rear admiral).

92. "To take charge of this post and all government property in view"

93. False. Turn **away** from the formation whenever possible.

94. Lieutenant general

95. States in the union, with the exception of the USS **Kearsarge** (BB-S)

96. Counties or parishes

97. Americans who have made significant contributions to the nation's heritage and states of the union

98. Amphibious operations requiring a diverse range of ships

99. Underway replenishment—the transfer of fuel, provisions and ammunition to operation units, allowing extended operation at sea

General—Answers

100. NROTC program

101. US Naval Forces, Mediterranean (redesignated the Sixth Task Fleet in 1948 and the current title in 1950)

102. Deck number, frame number, relation to centerline of the ship and use of the compartment

103. Twenty-four

104. The **Thetis Bay** (CVHA-1, commissioned July 1956)

105. False. Dolphins are awarded after completion of sub school **and** qualification in a boat.

106. The Portsmouth Navy Yard (Kittery, Maine)

107. Depth charges

108. Lockheed Electra

109. Harpoon

110. Trident

111. Trieste

112. The USS **Paulding** (DD-22)

113. The USS **Kearsarge**, under the command of Capt. J.B. Winslow (19 June 1864)

114. By dropping canisters of chlorsulphonic acid astern and by changing the mixture of air and fuel oil in the boilers

General—Answers

115. Pensacola, Florida

116. The uppermost complete deck is the main deck (a complete deck extends from side to side and from stem to stern).

117. Port Hueneme, California

118. Fireman

119. Drone Anti-Submarine Helicopter system

120. Annapolis, Maryland

121. The USS **Ticonderoga** (CG-47)

122. Thirty tons

123. The loading or off-loading of stores and material by helicopter

124. A nautical mile (by about 720 feet)

125. NATO's Standing Naval Force Atlantic

126. The Purple Heart

127. Little Creek, Virginia

128. The Naval Ordnance Station in Louisville, Kentucky. It is the major overhaul site for guns and missile launchers—everything from sixteen-inch guns on down.

129. Aviation Officer Candidate or Aviation Ordnance Chief; Pensacola, Florida

General—Answers

130. Ten days—the Liberty ship **Joseph N. Teal**, built by the Oregon Shipbuilding Corporation, Portland, Oregon

131. A sea-launched cruise missile

132. The ships inertial navigation system, a sophisticated device containing, among other components, accelerometers which detect changes in the direction of motion. The system output is a current latitude and longitude.

133. Submarine, missiles and support bases-namely Bangor, Washington, and Kings Bay, Georgia

134. Magnetic anomaly detection—a device which detects variations in the Earth's magnetic lines of force—used primarily for classification in ASW operations.

135. The USS **Will Rogers** (SSBN-659)

136. Iran

137. "Ayatollah Class"

138. The battleship **North Carolina** (BB-55)

139. Newport, Rhode Island

140. Forward and up to starboard, down and aft to port

141. Captain's Mast or simply, mast

142. The Executive Officer

General—Answers

143. An eight-wing structure overlooking the Pentagon—home to the Naval Military Personnel Command, Headquarters Marine Corps and many others

144. Indian Head, Maryland

145. Naval Amphibious Base Coronado, in San Diego, California

146. 1899

147. NAS Norfolk, Virginia

148. Nuclear attack subs such as the Los Angeles (SSN-688), Narwhal (SSN-671) and Sturgeon (SSN-637) classes

149. The partial vaccum in the fluid about a rapidly turning propellor. The vapor pockets form stream behind the blades and consume energy.

150. Altitude of the star above the horizon and time of observation to the nearest second

151. Combatant ships, combatant craft, auxiliary ships and service craft

152. The Enlisted Performance Record

153. The size of their main batteries, six-inch, eight-inch and twelve-inch respectively

154. Search and Rescue

155. NAS Miramar, California

156. The USS **Enterprise** (CVN-65)

General—Answers

157. Pensacola, Florida

158. New London, Connecticut

159. The USS **Spruance** (DD-963)

160. The USS **Perry** (DD-844)

161. Master commandant

162. Light Airborne Multipurpose System, a helicopter used as an extension of the parent ship's surveillance and attack system

163. The USS **Canberra** (CA-70)

164. The USS **Independence** (CV 62) on the left and the USS **Intrepid** (CVS 11) on the right

165. F3H-2M "Demon" armed with the "Sparrow" missile

166. F-14A "Tomcat"

167. S-2E "Tracker"

168. Heater intake

169. A new member of a "Hunter/Killer" ASW task force

170. OV-10 "Bronco"

171. Light Attack Squadron FOUR "Black Ponies"

172. Five-inch ZUNI air to ground rocket

General—Answers

173. He is a Landing Signal Officer (LSO). He is "waving off" an aircraft approaching for landing.

174. The USS **Bainbridge** (CGN-25)

175. The USS **Long Beach** (CGN-9)

176. RF8-A "Crusader"—photo-reconnaissance aircraft. The flag indicates that the unit (here VFP-62) has been awarded the Navy Unit Commendation.

177. The USS **Iowa** (BB-61)

178. The USS **George Washington** (SSBN-598)

179. Scout Observation Planes (SOC-1) shown in a diamond formation. These aircraft were launched from battleships and cruisers and were used to scout the enemy and observe gunfire.

Bibliography

Ageton, Arthur A., ed. **The Naval Officer's Guide.** 8th ed. Annapolis, Md.: U.S. Naval Institute, 1972.

Almanac of Naval Facts. Annapolis, Md.: U.S. Naval Institute, 1964.

Beck, Emily Morison, ed. **Bartlett's Familiar Quotations.** 15th ed. Boston: Little, Brown and Co., 1980.

Benford, Timothy B. **The World War II Quiz and Fact Book.** New York: Harper and Row, 1982.

Cagle, Malcom W. **The Naval Aviation Guide.** 2nd ed. Annapolis, Md.: U.S. Naval Institute, 1969.

Castano, J.B. **The Naval Officer's Uniform Guide.** Annapolis, Md.: U.S. Naval Institute, 1975.

Cole, J.A. **Lord Haw-Haw & William Joyce.** New York: Farrar, Straus & Giroux, 1965.

Deputy Chief of Naval Operations (Air Warfare) and Commander, Naval Air Systems Command. **United States Naval Aviation 1910-1980**. 3rd ed. U.S. Government Printing Office, 1980.

DOD Pam 1-20. **The Armed Forces Officer.** U.S. Government Printing Office, 1965.

Dunlap, G.D and Shufeldt, H.H., ed. **Dutton's Navigation and Piloting.** 12th ed. Annapolis, Md.: U.S. Naval Institute, 1969.

Friedman, Norman. **U.S. Destroyers.** Annapolis, Md.: U.S. Naval Institute, 1982.

Gunston, Bill. **F-4 PHANTOM.** New York: Charles Scribner's Sons, 1977.

Heinl, Robert D. **Dictionary of Military and Naval Quotations.** Annapolis, Md.: U.S. Naval Institute, 1966.

Keller, Charles L. and Robinson, Douglas H. **Up Ship!** Annapolis, Md.: US Naval Institute, 1982.

Kemp, Peter. **The Oxford Companion to Ships and the Sea.** London: Oxford University Press, 1976.

Kerrigan, Evans K. **American Badges and Insignia.** New York: Viking Press, 1967.

Knight, Austin. M. **Modern Seamanship.** 15th ed. New York: Van Nostrand Reinhold, 1972.

Lavalle, A.J.C. **The Tale of Two Bridges and the Battle for the Skies Over North Vietnam.** Vol. 1. U.S. Government Printing Office, 1976.

Lavalle, A.J.C. **Airpower and the 1972 Spring Invasion.** Vol. 1. U.S. Government Printing Office, 1976.

Lovette, Leland P. **Naval Customs, Traditions and Usage.** 3rd ed. Annapolis, Md.: U.S. Naval Institute, 1939.

McCombs, Don and Worth, Fred L. **World War II Superfacts.** New York: Warner Books, Inc., 1983.

Mersky, Peter B. and Polmar, Norman. **The Naval Air War in Vietnam.** Annapolis, Md.: The Nautical and Aviation Publishing Company of America, 1981.

Morison, Samuel Eliot. **The Oxford History of the American People.** New York: Oxford University Press, 1965.

Morison, Samuel Eliot. **The Two-Ocean War.** Boston: Little, Brown and Co., 1963.

Naval Education and Training Support Command. **Naval Orientation.** U.S. Government Printing Office, 1977.

NAVPERS 15047-A. **Navy Song Book.** Bureau of Naval Personnel, 1958.

Nevin, David. **The Pathfinders** (The Epic of Flight). Alexandria, Va: Time-Life, 1985.

Noel, J.V. Jr. **Division Officer's Guide.** 5th ed. Annapolis, Md.: U.S. Naval Institute, 1965.

Palmer, Joseph. **Jane's Dictionary of Naval Terms.** London: MacDonald and Janes, 1984.

Pater, Alan F. **United States Battleships.** Beverly Hills, Ca.: Monitor Book Co., 1968.

Pawlowski, Gareth L. **Flat-Tops and Fledglings**. South Brunswick and New York: A.S. Barnes and Co., 1971.

Polmar, Norman. **The American Submarine**. Annapolis, Md.: The Nautical Aviation Publishing Co., 1983.

Potter, E.B., ed. and Nimitz, Chester W., assoc. ed. **Seapower**. Englewood Cliffs, N.J.: Prentice-Hall, 1960.

Preston, Anthony. **Cruisers**. Englewood Cliffs, N.J.: Prentice-Hall, 1980.

Preston, Anthony. **Destroyers**. Englewood Cliffs, N.J.: Prentice-Hall, 1975.

Reef Points 1970-71. U.S. Naval Academy, Annapolis, Md.

Reynolds, Clark G. **Famous American Admirals**. New York: Van Nostrand, 1978.

Reynolds, Clark G. **The Fast Carriers, The Forging of an Air Navy.** Huntington, New York: Robert E Krieger Publishing Co., 1968.

Reynolds, Clark G. **The Carrier War** (The Epic of Flight). Alexandria, Va.: Time-Life, 1984.

Riley, David L. **Uncommon Valor.** Hopkinsville, Ky.: Eagle Printing, 1980.

Rogers, John G. **Origins of Sea Terms**. Boston: Nimrod Press, 1984.

Smith, S.E., ed. **The United States Navy in World War II.** New York: Ballantine, 1966.

Snouck-Hurgronje, Jan. ed. **Navigation and Operations.** Annapolis, Md.: U.S. Naval Institute, 1972.

Sweetman, Jack. **American Naval History**. Annapolis, Md.: U.S. Naval Institute, 1984.

The Fabulous Phantom. McDonnell Douglas Corp., 1978.

The Bluejackets Manual. 10th ed. Annapolis, Md.: U.S. Naval Institute, 1940.

United States Navy Flight Demonstration Squadron, **Blue Angels 1985**.

Walker, Bryce. **Fighting Jets** (The Epic of Flight). Alexandria, Va.: Time-Life, 1984.

Wedertz, Bill, ed. **The Bluejackets Manual.** 20th ed. Annapolis, Md.: U.S. Naval Institute, 1978.